GREAT

DISCOVER THE GREAT PLAINS

Series Editor: Richard Edwards, Center for Great Plains Studies

LINDA RAY PRATT

PLAINS

Literature

UNIVERSITY OF NEBRASKA PRESS   *Lincoln and London*

A Project of the Center for Great Plains Studies, University of Nebraska

"Christmas Mail" is reproduced by permission
of Ted Kooser. "At the Cancer Clinic," originally
published in *Delights and Shadows* (Port
Townsend WA: Copper Canyon Press, 2004),
also appears by permission of Ted Kooser.

Library of Congress Control Number: 2017039617

Set in Garamond Premier by Mikala R Kolander.

For my sister Amelia

CONTENTS

ILLUSTRATIONS

ACKNOWLEDGMENTS

My first acknowledgment must go to Rick Edwards, director of the Center for Great Plains Studies at the University of Nebraska–Lincoln. Rick conceptualized the series of short books under the heading of "Discover the Great Plains" and invited me to write the one on literature. Thanks are also due to Ted Kooser for permission to print two of his poems and to Rilla Askew for her generosity in talking with me and answering emails. Dale Stover and Chuck Trimble gave me valuable feedback on *Black Elk Speaks*. The archival staffs at the state historical societies of North Dakota, South Dakota, Missouri, Minnesota, and Nebraska, as well as at Marquette University, deserve a special nod of appreciation. The research of my colleagues in the Departments of English and History across the University of Nebraska system was enormously helpful. Writing this book gave me a fresh appreciation of the depth of work on the Great Plains that has come out of the faculties on our campuses, the Center for Great Plains Studies, and the University of Nebraska Press. My greatest personal indebtedness is to my husband, Bill Pratt, who is a historian of the Great Plains. Our almost-daily conversations about the literature and history of the region were only matched by the constant borrowing of his books. His own research and historiographical knowledge of the Great Plains provided a private research library and staff just footsteps from my desk.

GREAT PLAINS LITERATURE

CHAPTER ONE

Under Spacious Skies

I reached some plains so vast, that I did not find their limit anywhere
I went, although I traveled over them for more than 300 leagues . . .
with no more land marks than if we had been swallowed up by the sea.
—Spanish explorer, Coronado, 1541

One of the most beloved patriotic songs of the United States,
"America the Beautiful," paints this iconic image of the nation:

O beautiful for spacious skies,
For amber waves of grain,
For purple mountain majesties
Above the fruited plain!

In 1893 the expansive view of the Great Plains from atop the
"purple mountain," Pikes Peak, inspired Katherine Lee Bates
to write the poem that became the lyrics of "America the
Beautiful." This Wellesley College English professor with a
summer teaching job at Colorado College took a train across
the "amber waves of grain" of Kansas to Colorado Springs and
climbed Pikes Peak, the pink granite mountain dotted with
blue columbine flowers. This description of the Great Plains
is sung so often that the actual reference is largely lost in the
rote performance.

Despite being enshrined in our national hymn to America's
majestic landscape, many people don't much care for "spacious

Fig. 1. Northern Great Plains with abandoned farmhouse. Courtesy of photographer Bill Pratt from his personal collection.

skies" and "amber waves of grain." In contemporary parlance, this landscape is sometimes dismissed as "the flyover zone." The irony of the reverence for the images in the song and the disregard for the actual view is emblematic of the misunderstandings and mixed messages about the history and culture of the real place. For some, the region is just empty space where nothing much ever happens.

Yet four things stand out in American history as defining experiences whose impact continues to shape the culture today: the American Revolution; slavery and the Civil War; the settling of the frontier; and the conquering of the Indian nations. Two of these, the settling of the frontier and the conquering of the Indian nations, played out their most dramatic chapters on the Great Plains. In Canadian history, the westward movement into the plains and the defeat of French interests in the Seven Years' War (1754–63), known in the United States as the

French and Indian War, are important defining episodes that influenced Canadian development, including relations with the indigenous people. The region holds within its history and cultures some of the nation's most bitter and inspiring stories of triumph and betrayal, democracy and intolerance, wealth and poverty. Canadian history is not as violent as American, and Canada generally had less destructive relations with First Nations people than did the United States. The ironies of the region, however, were there from the beginning: the expanse of "free" land that required the removal of the people who already lived there; the marketing of the arid prairie as a garden where the rain would follow the plow; a rich soil but a scarce rainfall; the building of frontier communities in which neighbor helped neighbor unless they were of a different ethnic origin or religious belief. Even the long geological evolutions were full of incongruities—once a great inland sea, a near tropical place where prehistoric animals roamed, the plains were reshaped by a massive glaciation into grassland where some of the first white settlers reported that not even a bird sang. Fossil beds across the plains yield bones of fish, camels, elephantine mammoths, and ancient peoples who apparently migrated to the region over the ice bridges from northern Asia. The first people arrived more than fifteen thousand years ago.

The many lives of the topography we call today the "Great Plains" raise the question of just where it is and how it is different from other plains. By most measurements, the region runs from the Canadian Prairies in Alberta, Saskatchewan, and Manitoba down through West Texas and New Mexico to the Rio Grande. The southwestern section of the Great Plains—known as the Llano Estacado, or "Staked Plains," so called originally by the Spanish explorers because the plains end in a series of steep cliffs—is the driest and flattest of all. The *Encyclopedia of the Great Plains* includes a delightfully

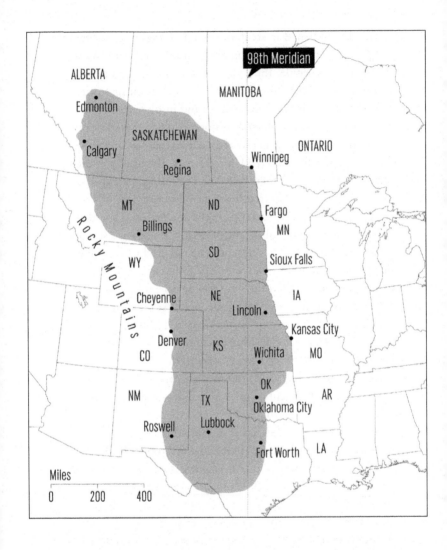

Fig. 2. Map of the Great Plains labeled "The Great Plains region as defined by the Encyclopedia of the Great Plains," from the *Encyclopedia of the Great Plains*, 2004, xiv. Courtesy of the Center for Great Plains Studies, University of Nebraska.

squiggly map showing the numerous definitions various cartographers have used. What is remarkable about this map is how much agreement there is and how little difference the variations register. For the purposes of this book, I shall use the map on which the Center for Great Plains Studies at the University of Nebraska–Lincoln settled.

The demarcations of the Great Plains are often drawn by mountain ranges and rivers. In Canada the great forests are another border. In places, the plains are visually dramatic, as they were for Bates at Pikes Peak. Landing at the Denver airport from the east, you see below you the barrenness of the plains, dotted here and there with green circles of center-pivot irrigation; rising ahead of you are the Rocky Mountains. Descending from Glacier National Park on the Going-to-the-Sun Road toward East Glacier Park Village, Montana, the mountains suddenly end, and the Great Plains spread before you as far as the eye can see. In 1804 Lewis and Clark met with the Otoe Indians on what they called the Council Bluffs. From this Iowa hill they could look over the Missouri River to the Great Plains that lay ahead of them.

Not all the lines of demarcation are so precise—that is, unless you are traveling the territory at ground level. One of the enchantments of the Great Plains is that once you have seen them, you will always know when you are there. Minnesota, Iowa, and Missouri are not the Great Plains; the Dakotas, Nebraska, and Kansas are. How can a river, even a wide one like the Missouri, make such a topographical change? The hills on the east side are often higher, the rocks bigger, the trees more plentiful, the creeks and streams more frequent. The glaciers did not have their way with them as easily as they cut through the plains. The earmarks of the Great Plains are aridity, wind, few trees, wind, grasses, empty spaces—did I mention wind? Nature is all extremes—in wind, in drought, in hot, in cold.

Fig. 3. Where the pavement ends, 2008. Location is near 170th and Fort Street, Omaha, looking west. Courtesy of photographer Chris Beran, from his personal collection.

In dazzling sunsets, in vast blue skies, in blinding blizzards, in tornadic clouds. How could we not love it? As the poet Mark Sanders wrote, "Were the weather any different / it would not be ours" ("Plain Sense"). Perhaps the ironies and contradictions in the history and culture cut so deeply because plains people live in a zone in which nothing much sets up the barriers that might moderate the extremes.

Climate and landscape play on the psyche, stirring two conflicting responses to the plains environment. Some find the space isolating and fearful; others find it liberating. Canadians often discuss the "garrison mentality" that seeks protection from a threatening environment by adhering to the group and its rules. Yet many longtime residents of the Great Plains speak of the *need* for the open horizon before them. N. Scott Momaday wrote that "the Kiowas reckoned their stature by the distance they could see, and they were bent and blind in the wilderness." A former student returned for a visit after completing his basic training for the U.S. Marines in Parris Island, South Carolina. He told me he hated it. "The harsh training?" I asked. "God, no. That was fine. It was the trees. Trees everywhere. I felt I was smothering in them!" A professional woman who must work in urban Omaha lives on the western suburban edge of the city so that she can jog every morning to where her street plays out and the cornfields begin. "My favorite sign is 'Pavement Ends,'" she told me.

The Native tribes feared that the whites would fill up the land. Many of the settlers also thought that was the future, but most of the plains remains sparsely populated. The rural population is in decline, and some rural counties claim fewer than half a dozen people per square mile.

Those who make their living off the land require vast acreages, whether to farm or ranch or frack for oil. The few cities sprawl outward and not upward, because the land is there to develop. The isolation of rural life deepens as the changes in farming, transportation, and the aspirations of young people continue to empty out the little towns. That fabled little house on the prairie is more likely today to house two aging adults whose grown children have left the farm, rather than a boisterous family of kids and pet calves. The new residents who show up in towns are often Latinos. True to the darker side of frontier tradition, these "others" typically do not find a warm welcome, although their boost to rural population is arguably the one thing saving many towns from withering away. Across the plains, almost all the population growth is in the cities on the edges of the region—Winnipeg, Sioux Falls, Omaha, Kansas City, Lubbock, Denver, Calgary. What will be the effect of urban life on the psyche and the culture of a region developed under spacious skies and amber waves of grain when most of the population lives in cities? How far will they have to run to find that "Pavement Ends" sign?

A region so sharply defined by its geography and history was bound to produce a literary culture absorbed in telling its stories. There is a difference between a region being a setting and the region driving the story. This commentary on the literature of the Great Plains will focus on those writers whose work has an integral relationship to place and history. The reader who has picked up this book is assumed to have a curiosity about the Great Plains as a place and an interest in what the literature tells us about the region. There is a rich bounty of such Great Plains literature, especially when we consider how relatively short in historic time there has been a culture that could produce literary work. Many of the region's most distinguished authors knew people who remembered the events narrated in their novels. The literature discussed in this study was written in the twentieth century, though much of it is set in the nineteenth. Black Elk's memories are of events in his youth and climax in his account of the massacre at Wounded Knee in 1890. Willa Cather was born in 1873, Ole Rölvaag in 1876, and John Neihardt in 1881. In the Canadian Prairie Provinces, novelist Margaret Laurence attempts to recapture the past through the myths and memory of characters who recall, and invent, an earlier time. Cather's first novel is published in 1912. Rölvaag's epic trilogy of the settlement of the Great Plains begins to appear in 1927.

Almost two hundred years of American literature had been amassed before the literature of the Great Plains began. William Bradford's *Of Plymouth Plantation* was written between 1630 and 1651, and African American poet Phillis Wheatley published her poems in 1773. Hawthorne, Emerson, Thoreau, Fuller, Whitman, Dickinson, and Melville had all died before the end of the nineteenth century. Distant in both time and geography from eastern and southern literary traditions and the Revolutionary and Civil Wars, which dominated the history of those regions, plains writers were free from the thematic inheritance that had preoccupied much nineteenth-century literature. The large numbers of immigrants also brought to the plains many literary traditions from other lands. The Great Plains did not need to search for a "meter-making argument," as Emerson called for in 1844, because no school of plains writers had been trying for almost one hundred years to capture the realities of a new and different nation through British literary traditions.

In a survey of eighteenth- and nineteenth-century American literature, there is almost nothing about the Great Plains except Washington Irving's *Tour of the Prairies* in 1835, an account of a trip he took to the "prairie" that went no farther than eastern Oklahoma, and James Fenimore Cooper's *The Prairie*. This novel recounting the last chapter in the life of Natty Bumppo, hero of the Leatherstocking Tales, was written in 1827 by a New Yorker who never saw the Great Plains. Yet Cooper deserves a mention in this literary introduction for the profundity of his insight and imagination. His "rolling prairie" was "far beyond the usual limits of civilized habitations" and extended "with . . . little diversity of character to the bases of the Rocky Mountains." Cooper adds that "the meager herbage of the prairie promised nothing in favor of a hard and unyielding soil over which the vehicles rattled." Though he described the famously shallow Platte River as "swift and turbid" and the dense and tall prairie grass as "meager herbage," Cooper caught something of the vastness of the Great Plains. He knew little about the people who were moving into it, however, or the living conditions that early settlement demanded. We can hardly fault Cooper for his deficiencies of understanding when he wrote this novel in the 1820s since there were very few settlers to describe it. It was not until the 1850s, and later in 1862 with the Homestead Act, that the flow of families westward significantly increased.

The literary portraits of the Great Plains begin with the journals of explorers. In 1690–92 a young man named Henry Kelsey was the first European to explore the Canadian prairies and record bison and grasslands. Kelsey was sent into the wilderness by the Hudson's Bay Company to encourage the Indians to trade with them, a task at which he was apparently successful. Kelsey was quite young, seventeen perhaps, and his assignment was nothing like that of Lewis and Clark, whose president had given specific directives to record all they saw of the unexplored territory. Kelsey's journal was essentially lost to Canadian history in the Hudson's Bay Company archives until the twentieth century. Much later and better known are the journals of Meriwether Lewis and William Clark, written during the 1804–6 expedition from St. Louis, Missouri, across the country to the Pacific coast. Americans first read a version of the journals in 1814, and one member of the Corps of Discovery also published his own account. Undoubtedly, the public was very interested in this expedition to chart the newly acquired Louisiana Purchase (1803) and its findings about the West, though it is hard to know just how much of the richness of the actual text of Lewis and Clark was the source of nineteenth-century understanding.

Accounts of the explorations of the Great Plains by Maj. Stephan H. Long and Zebulon Pike in 1819–20 were popular with the public and likely more influential on early conceptions of the area. Major Long first labeled the plains the "Great American Desert" and declared it unfit for cultivation. The journals of Lewis and Clark as a whole were not published until 1904–5. In 2001 Gary E. Moulton's thirteen volumes of a complete edition was published, and in 2003 a one-volume abridgement appeared as *The Lewis and Clark Journals*. Any reader who gets thoroughly hooked on the saga of Lewis and Clark will want to browse the many volumes that Moulton magnificently edited. The numerous illustrations and scientific details in the complete edition are wonderful to behold and deepen our regard for the thoroughness with which Lewis and Clark endeavored to meet the expectations set out for them by President Thomas Jefferson.

In many ways, the journals of Lewis and Clark are the West's equivalent to classic early American works by authors William Bradford, *Of Plymouth Plantation* (1606–46); William Byrd, *The History of the Dividing Line betwixt Virginia and North Carolina* (1728–36); and William Bartram, *Travels through North and South Carolina, Georgia, East and West Florida* (1773–77). All are firsthand accounts of the earliest recorded history of a region, and Byrd and Bartram in particular share with Lewis and Clark the interest in recording observations about Indians, plants, and geography. All have the freshness of being original documents, and all record significant moments in American history.

Moulton calls the journals of Lewis and Clark "a national treasure" that will remain "for all time our American epic." Patricia Limerick calls the myth of the "Old Frontier" America's "creation story," the place where the virtues and values of the country took shape. John Neihardt also connected the story of settlement of the Great Plains to literary traditions of the classical epics. Epics of discovery and conquest are often the first literary representations of wars between cultures, complete with heroic actions against terrible odds, strange new dangers, long periods of suffering and conflict, and courageous triumphs over seemingly insurmountable troubles. They must have a cast of memorable characters, an episodic narrative, and a hero or heroes whose personal abilities lead to the victory over all forces. Surely the heroic Lewis and Clark; the vital heroine, Sacagawea; the fearsome and noble Indians; the various scoundrels and good Samaritans; the many adventures on the river and through the mountains; and the wonder of the Pacific Ocean on the western coast all fit the requirements of an epic.

As they traveled up the Missouri River bordering the Kansas and Nebraska territory, Lewis and Clark responded to their first views of the Great Plains with delight and enthusiasm. On July 12, 1804, climbing an artificial mound that he identified as a grave, Clark saw before him "one of the most pleasing prospects [he] ever beheld." He describes a "Butifull River of Clear water . . . a leavel and extensive Meadow, as far as [he] could See, . . . The bottom land . . . covered with Grass and rich weeds & flours, interspersed with Copses of the Osage Plumb." On July 19 he "Came Suddenly into an open and bound less Prarie":

> I Say bound less because I could not See the extent of the plain in any Derection, the timber appeared to be confined to the River Creeks & Small branches, this Prarie was Covered with grass about 18 Inches or 2 feat high and contained little of any thing else . . . This prospect was So Sudden & entertaining that I forgot the object of my prosute [pursuit] and turned my attention to the Variety which presented themselves to my view.

On July 30, camped near the Council Bluff, Clark continued his observations: "Capt. Lewis and my Self walked in the Prarie on the top of the Bluff and observed the most butifull prospects imagionable, this Prarie is Covered with grass about 10 to 12 Inch high, . . . the River may be Seen for a great Distance both above & below meandering thro." In these early days of the journey, the "Prarie" seemed full of animals for food, berries, plums, clear water, rich land, green grass, and natural beauty.

Farther along, they would see thousands of buffalo. Many of the Indian tribes were friendly, and Lewis and Clark became quite adept in dealing with them. Before the journey would end, they would find food more scarce, the natives less friendly, and the plains less "entertaining"; but they never really abandoned their enthusiastic appreciation of the land and people they met along the way.

Many of the early settlers who made their way into the Great Plains echoed the responses we see in Lewis and Clark. Later writers express the same unbounded enthusiasm and near despair, defeat and victory, idealism and sobering realities that we see in the journals of Lewis and Clark. As Moulton notes, however, one important difference is that Lewis and Clark never strayed far from the river. Only the settlers who came later learned what it meant to clear that grassland and put in a crop. Only the settlers had to make do with homes made of the prairie sod because there were no trees for lumber. And as the settlers came in ever increasing numbers, only then did the indigenous tribes have to confront the terrible tragedy their arrival ultimately meant for Indian survival. The literature of the Great Plains tells a story that both resonates with that of early American literature of settlement and exploration and differs from it in its geography of vast plains, intemperate extremes of climate, and the still-unresolved tragedy of Indian wars. This study will reveal to us both the pioneering struggles needed for these territories to become bona fides of their nation and the legacy of that past as it plays out today in a contemporary society that wants both to forget and to remember.

Choosing a handful of books to illustrate the best and most pertinent literary works from so vast an area as the Great Plains is about as scientific as a roll of the dice. Both Canada and the United States have rich literary histories, and authors like Willa Cather or Wallace Stegner might have nearly a dozen books from which one could choose. Laura Ingalls Wilder expanded her books about life in a little house on the prairie through five generations. Larry McMurtry's stories of the old West and modern Texas are widely known through popular novels and film adaptations. Margaret Laurence and Louise Erdrich have numerous award-winning books. Bearing in mind the readers who seek an introduction to the literature of a region, I have picked some of the best-written books that also delve deeply into some aspect of Great Plains culture and history. The story that Lewis and Clark began continues in chapter 2 with the literary accounts of the first people through the memories in *Black Elk Speaks* (1932), Zitkala-Ša's *American Indian Stories* (1921), and N. Scott Momaday's mythic *The Way to Rainy Mountain* (1969). Nicholas Black Elk, an Oglala Sioux who lived through the most tragic days of the Indian wars, chose to tell his story to John Neihardt, who immortalized it as *Black Elk Speaks*. Zitkala-Ša's stories of life on the reservation and in the Indian schools powerfully portray the humiliation and suffering that accompanied acculturation. Momaday re-creates with myth and history the migration of the Kiowas from Montana to the reservation in Oklahoma.

Aside from the indispensable *Black Elk Speaks*, the next most obvious choice was the great saga of the early white settlers by Norwegian writer Ole Edvart Rölvaag. Chapter 3 explores his trilogy of novels telling the story of the Holm family in an epic of the first white cultivation of the land and the building of a community. Of the three novels—*Giants in the Earth*, *Peder Victorious*, and *Their Fathers' God*, first published in America in 1925, 1928, and 1931, respectively—the undisputed greatest is *Giants in the Earth*. Per Hans's enchantment with all that the untouched prairie seemed to promise is countered by his wife Beret's fear and horror at this empty but threatening plain. In the next two novels, their sons break from the Norwegian traditions so dear to their mother and continue the inevitable process of acculturation.

If Rölvaag writes the epic of pioneer settlement, Willa Cather writes its elegy. Chapter 4 will look at how class and gender bias emerge and work against success and personal freedom in this new society. Cather profoundly admires the courage and endurance of the pioneers, but she is not sentimental about what the following generations are doing. In *O Pioneers!*, *My Ántonia*, and *A Lost Lady*, she portrays three women heroines who embody some of the best of the pioneer spirit but whose fates also reveal the darker side of immigrant settlement. Ethnic discrimination and class differentiation quickly arise when even the smallest of towns get organized and the bones of a society and economy are formed.

The promise of a good living, which so much free land seemed to hold, led to acute disappointment and failure for many people. The climate had many weapons against productivity, and the men who controlled the money did, too. Both in the Prairie Provinces of Canada and in the United States, the Great Depression was deepened by drought and dust. The acute financial difficulties of plains farmers during such hard times sparked disillusionment and dissent. Protest movements and radical groups played a significant role in the history of the region from the late 1800s throughout the farm crisis of the 1980s. The Populists, the Nonpartisan League, the Socialists, and the Communists all organized with some degree of success the anger and despair of "the people."

Chapter 5 will look at three writers who focus on the misery and ruin that accompanied the Great Depression on the plains. John Steinbeck's *The Grapes of Wrath* (1939) is the most famous Depression epic. It starts with memorable scenes of the Joads in Oklahoma, but most of the novel is about Dust Bowl migrants in California. Steinbeck was not from the Great Plains, and there are many other writers more clearly anchored in the region who could chart the long despair of losing one's land. For most, it was not a quick or passive process, and these writers factored the economics and political dissent as part of their subject. Several of the most successful writers were women. Lois Phillips Hudson's *The Bones of Plenty* gives us a more realistic and more typical story of the wheat farmers of North Dakota. Unlike the romanticized Joad family, George and Rachel Custer deal with the stress and anger that tear at their marriage and family ties as well as their farming. Mari Sandoz presents a more political analysis of the politicians and financial powers that thwarted the efforts of farmers and workers to get help to survive. While not her best work, *Capital City* attempts to tease out the connections between the class with money and political power and the exploitation of the poor. Her account of the people of "Franklin, Kanewa," delivers a sting to the powers in control.

Not all the history and culture of the Great Plains occurred in rural areas. Even Laura Ingalls Wilder's *Little House on the Prairie* is followed in volume seven with the *Little Town on the Prairie*. The immigrants were not all western European Catholics and Protestants, either. Chapter 6 will look at the stories that reflect events in the cities where the majority of the population now lives and where the diversity of the people is most evident. Tillie Olsen's *Yonnondio* recounts the misery that the Holbrook family finds in a meatpacking city like Omaha where they hope to find a fresh start. Meridel Le Sueur's *The Girl* puts aside many of the stereotypes of "farm girl goes to the city" to explore what young women find there. Rilla Askew's *Fire in Beulah* graphically exposes the nexus between the hunger for money—oil money in this case—and the brutal racism that resulted in the 1921 race riot in Tulsa, Oklahoma.

Chapter 7 will explore the interplay of the past as it continues to play out in the future. Poet Ted Kooser reveals the emotional lives of "ordinary" people and the beauty of places around him in small towns that can fill a life with richness of meaning. For him this is not a dying world. Kent Haruf's novels in the fictional town of Holt, Colorado, also embody life in small towns today. His fiction is like an update of Cather's many versions of Red Cloud but with a much deeper sense of grace for the human condition. The lingering damage to Native American lives on the reservation is expressed in the novels of Louise Erdrich. *The Plague of Doves* tells in innovative narrative form how two terrible crimes against whites and Native Americans continue to play out in their interconnected lives. Margaret Laurence's *The Diviners*, set in her fictionalized town of Manawaka, Manitoba, also explores the mythic pasts that both the Métis characters and the Scot immigrants create to counter the realities of a modern life that offers them little respect. These writers and many of lesser fame continue to explore the themes that have shaped the literature of the Great Plains.

Literature on the Great Plains has never been more prolific than it is now, and there are numerous works with the promise of lasting merit. The past sometimes seems to haunt the present for these writers as they look at an uncertain future. In *Where the Bluebird Sings to the Lemonade Springs* Wallace Stegner warns writers against the tendency toward nostalgia or bitterness, noting that "we began to regret the wilderness almost before we invaded it, and to yearn for the past before we had one." This warning seems even more necessary as we face significant transforming change in the shaping elements of Great Plains culture—agriculture, population shifts, climate, politics. Demographically, a once dominantly rural world is rapidly becoming a dominantly urban one, and even the fundamentals of land and water could be at risk. These new authors face the challenge of how to use the traditions of the literature of the last century as a new environment and culture emerge.

CHAPTER TWO

Fencing In the First People

They told us that they wanted only to use a little land, as much as a wagon would take between the wheels; but our people knew better. And when you look about you now, you can see what it was they wanted.
—Black Elk

There are many stories of the first people on the Great Plains, told in many languages, but almost all of them have the same ending: the reservation. Archeological evidence in the region suggests that Native people have inhabited the Great Plains for at least fifteen thousand years. Population numbers are harder to determine, but some estimates place the population of Plains Indians at seventy-five thousand in 1850. We know from the formal explorations of Lewis and Clark and later Stephan H. Long that they met with many sizable tribes in the path of their journeys across the plains. At his 1819 meeting at the Council Bluffs with tribal *leaders* from the local tribes, Long counted "about one hundred Ottoes, seventy Missouries, and fifty or sixty Ioways." At an earlier meeting with the Konzas and Osage, his count was about 175 leaders and chiefs. The plains were anything but empty before the white settlers arrived.

Treaties from as early as 1722 had acknowledged the presence of Indian nations, and in 1832 the Supreme Court ruled in *Worcester v. Georgia* that the relationship between the

United States and Indian nations was that of one nation to another. The pressure of the westward expansion continued, however, and little respect was paid to *Worcester v. Georgia*, even by President Andrew Jackson. In U.S. history literally hundreds of treaties with Indian nations were recognized by the Department of State. On the Great Plains, Indian lands were diced and cut throughout the rest of the century to accommodate the expansion of settlers, miners, and railroads. From the earliest encounters with white fur traders, contact with Europeans was an unmitigated disaster for Native peoples. Smallpox, measles, and other contagious diseases first ravaged Indian tribes, killing as many as 80 percent of the tribe in some areas. From 1830 on, a series of wars, treaties, and policies pushed the Indians into more remote areas and smaller reservations. In his book *American Carnage: Wounded Knee, 1890*, Jerome Greene reports that at the end of the wars against the Plains Indians, the count of Sioux in all its configurations was about thirty-nine thousand people. The many "trails of tears" of Indian removal followed diverse paths across the country, most of them muddied with blood as well as tears.

The stories *about* Plains Indians became the stuff of Wild West shows and later of western movies. The stereotype of feathered warriors in war paint riding ponies at breakneck speed across the prairies to attack covered wagons is all too familiar. The stories *by* Plains Indians relate a considerably different tale. Three native voices representing different times and experiences stand out in the literature of Native American experience on the Great Plains. They are those of Black Elk, Zitkala-Ša, and N. Scott Momaday. Through the transcriptions of his life as told to John G. Neihardt, Nicholas Black Elk tells of the spiritual and historical worlds he experienced and his ill-fated mission to bring the two spheres together to save his people.

Fig. 4. Nicholas Black Elk wearing festive attire in 1937. Photograph by W. Ben Hunt. Courtesy of Marquette University Archives, Bureau of Catholic Indian Missions Records, ID 01287.

Zitkala-Ša's *American Indian Stories* (1921) draws from life on the reservation and the conqueror's efforts to strip Indian culture by removing Indian children to schools where a brutal program of acculturation was enforced. In a more recent time, Scott Momaday's *The Way to Rainy Mountain* (1969) tells in myth, history, and remembrance the chronicle of the Kiowas from life in the Montana territory to the reservation in Oklahoma.

Black Elk Speaks has been the most praised and influential account we have of a life lived during the crucible of years that resulted in the "selling" of the Black Hills, the removal of Sioux people to reservations, and the massacre at Wounded Knee in 1890. Black Elk, an Oglala Lakota (Sioux), was an eyewitness to some of the most important events in plains history from 1863–90. He was also a visionary whose account of his life reveals the spiritual framework at the center of Lakota beliefs about nature and the cosmos. In his introduction, Vine Deloria Jr. calls *Black Elk Speaks* "a North American bible of all tribes," and for many contemporary Native Americans, it is an invaluable source of inspiration and information about the spiritual life of their ancestors before the forced "Christianizing" on the reservations and in the Indian schools. The book is equally important for other readers who want to get beyond stereotypes in their understanding of a Native American way of ordering the world and the unabated tragic costs to Indian people of white settlement in the Great Plains.

The account of how *Black Elk Speaks* came into existence is itself remarkable. The text we have as Black Elk's story is a tale within a tale within a tale. Black Elk, literate in his own language, knew only a few English words, which he had picked up traveling in Buffalo Bill's Wild West Show. John G. Neihardt, the sympathetic writer who translates into literary English

Fig. 5. John Neihardt. Photograph by Ron Nicodemus. Courtesy of the John G. Neihardt Trust.

what he believes Black Elk to have said, knew only a few words of Lakota.

Black Elk was an elderly man almost seventy years old when he told his story to Neihardt in May 1931. His life had been that of a holy man and healer. Born in 1863, he had lived through the Battle of the Little Bighorn, the near annihilation of the buffalo, the slaughter at Wounded Knee, and the surrender and removal to the reservations. Black Elk was also a mystic who wanted to tell his story so that his vision would not die with him.

Black Elk felt that Neihardt had been sent to him to learn what he knew and preserve his vision in written words. Both men believed in the power of mystical experience, albeit from different cultures, and Neihardt was prepared to listen to Black Elk's account without cynicism or condescension. Neihardt brought his daughter, Enid, who was a stenographer, to take down what the interpreter said, and Black Elk designated his son, Ben, to be his interpreter. As Black Elk spoke, Ben translated. Enid recorded Ben's translation, and later, Neihardt tried to capture in prose the elegance, the rhythms, and the metaphoric phrasing he heard in the spoken sound of Black Elk's voice and the transcript of the steno notes of his daughter. Enid's typed transcript of her notes was published in *The Sixth Grandfather: Black Elk's Teachings Given to John G. Neihardt* by Raymond DeMallie in 1984. This book allowed scholars to compare the transcript and the stylistic additions Neihardt made in his prose account. Scholars vary in their judgements about how much of the text is Black Elk and how much is Neihardt and about how much that affects the value readers assign to the book. One's answers to these questions may depend on why one reads *Black Elk Speaks* as much as it does on how bothersome one may find Neihardt's stylistic emendations. The one certainty is that *Black Elk Speaks*, no matter where the voices

Fig. 6. Black Elk in 1931. Photograph by John G. Neihardt. John G. Neihardt (1881–1973) Papers, ca. 1858–1974. Courtesy of the Western Historical Manuscript Collection, State Historical Society of Missouri.

diverge or blend, is a powerful story of a Native American life and spiritual vision during one of the most tumultuous times in Native American history.

Black Elk (Heȟáka Sápa in Lakota) was only nine years old when he had the vision that would guide his life. The boy lay ill with a high fever during which he had a vision revealing his destiny. The dream unfolds with a series of twelve horses that take him to the four directions of the winds and the sky and the earth. The spiritual Six Grandfathers give the boy the wooden cup full of water and the sky, and they place a bow and arrows in his hands, symbols of the power to create and the power to destroy. As he moves across the skies in his journey, a rainbow spreads over him, everything in the cosmos dances, and "the whole wide circle of the day [is] beautiful and green, with all fruits growing and all things kind and happy." The vision also foretells the great troubles for his nation but gives him the power to heal.

Ultimately, this mystical experience takes him to the highest mountain at the center of the earth where he sees "the whole hoop of the world." When the vision ends, the Six Grandfathers have given him the cup, the bow and arrows, the stick that sprouts branches and leaves, the pipe, and the hoop—symbols of life, destruction, peace, and the oneness of all living things. His vision contains both beauty and terror, but the beauty is so great "that nothing anywhere could keep from dancing." When the boy wakes, he feels well but very sad because he cannot articulate the feelings or the meaning or revisit the place he had been. This vision never quite leaves Black Elk, and his life is punctuated by recurrences of premonitions and voices warning him of dangers. When he is seventeen, some scenes from his vision are dramatized before the people in what must have been a spectacular ceremony, complete with horses and virgins and the cup, the bow, the herbs, the flowering stick, the holy pipe, and the nation's hoop. After that, his people know of his special powers. At this point in his life, Black Elk believes that he will be able to realize the destiny for which the vision has prepared him.

This brief summary barely hints at the experience his words portray or the length and complexity of Black Elk's dreams. Vision quests were an integral part of Lakota spiritual practice, and every young man was expected to undergo a vision quest as part of his spiritual initiation to adulthood. Black Elk had other visions but none that had more impact on him than the one he had as a boy. The symbols and meaning of his vision are consistent with other accounts of Lakota beliefs, and his account is highly valued for its embodiment of Native American religion. For some readers and scholars, both within the Native American community and far beyond it, the book constitutes one of the most authentic works in American religious writing. DeMallie has carefully examined the original transcript made by Enid Neihardt and found that it was "not foreign to Lakota culture" but that Black Elk was more "ecumenical" in his vision than was typical.

Some Lakota people may feel that the "ecumenical" approach to understanding and appreciating Black Elk's vision is another colonizing framework from white culture, but the power of his vision for readers outside the Lakota community is undeniable. DeMallie calls Black Elk's symbols "pan cultural archetypes," and indeed they are consistent with an ancient spiritual symbolism that was transmuted into contemporary religions across the globe. Perhaps what gives Black Elk's vision ecumenical significance is that it expresses the ageless desire to know the mysteries of the universe, and it does so with the symbols and ceremonies through which humanity has long configured its quest for divine insight into the reality of life and death, time and eternity. Some scholars have interpreted these ageless symbols as evidence of Black Elk's Christian faith or influence, but that is probably a mistake and certainly not necessary since Christianity itself appropriates the same ageless symbols. The symbols in Black Elk's vision are similar to those that originated in the ancient fertility myths that were the beginnings of religion, remnants of which continue to exist in modern religions and accounts of visionary experience. Symbols such as the cup, the "tree of life," the star, and the hoop exist in both religious and occult practices, such as those associated with tarot cards, which legend says were used in predicting the flooding of the Nile in ancient Egypt. Dancing itself symbolizes the unity of the mortal and immortal, the ideal and the real, as we see in W. B. Yeats's brilliant metaphor, "How can we know the dancer from the dance?"

Late nineteenth-century comparative mythographers, notably Sir James G. Frazer in his multivolume study, *The Golden Bough* (1890), gathered from across many cultures a set of rituals and symbols common to "pagan mythologies" (religions that we no longer believe). The rituals were associated with fertility, healing, and explaining the observable phenomena of the natural world, including the origins of life and the meaning of death. Frazer traced the meanings and symbols of these ceremonies as they evolved into modern religions such as Christianity.

Others, such as Jessie Weston, examined the evolution of ancient key symbols like the cup with the holy grail or the tree of life with the cross of Christianity. Weston's *From Ritual to Romance* (1920) includes a chapter titled "The Medicine Man," whom she says is always both a healer and a priest, as was Black Elk. The medicine man she discusses, however, is in a poem about the healing power of herbs in the *Rig-Veda*, a collection of poems and songs in Sanskrit dating at least back to 2000 B C. The healer-priest who can cure sickness and save the people makes its way into Christianity in the figure of

Jesus. The boy Black Elk could not have known of this long evolution of religious thought, and yet his vision combines the ancient and seemingly universal symbols with those that are integral to Lakota spiritual practices. Symbols such as the cup, the branch, and the hoop (circle) are as old as the earliest evidence of spiritual myths about the origin of life. Other symbols, such as the horses, the eagle, and the bow arise from Lakota life on the plains.

Lakota culture attaches great significance to dreams as visionary experience, but it is also true that Black Elk describes in his dream a pattern similar to that in mysticism in many other spiritual traditions. The interior map of mystical experience is that the seeker or pilgrim or quester, in a dark night of the soul, is drawn up and out of selfhood in a moment out of time in which the presence of absolute reality is felt. This process is often preceded by a purification of the flesh, including sickness and fever, and is a critical moment of spiritual growth and enlightenment. A vision of the absolute is experienced in symbolic ways that are not easily articulated because they are beyond the spatial and time boundaries of our ordinary awareness. When the mystical moment is gone, the mystic is alone with the inexpressible experience and feels sadness and a longing to recapture the transcendence that has changed her or his life.

Some version of this basic pattern is present in accounts of mystical experiences from such classic religious mystics as St. John of the Cross (San Juan de la Cruz) to the secular mysticism of the poet Tennyson, who feels his soul "whirl'd / About empyreal heights of thought" until he comes on "that which is, and ca[tches] / The deep pulsations of the world, / Aeonian music measuring out / The steps of Time—the shocks of Chance— / The blows of Death" (*In Memoriam*, section 95). Black Elk's description of the beauty and terror of his moment whirling above the earth in oneness with the powers of life and death, and the sadness that haunts him when he wakes and is separated from the experience, unable to express it to anyone, are authentic to the universal traditions of mystical literature.

The teachings of the Six Grandfathers and the gifts they give Black Elk to accomplish his destiny are also a heavy burden. He is told, "On earth a nation you shall make live, for yours shall be the power ... what sickens there you shall make well ... you shall have the power to destroy a people's foes." When he sees below him a village of his nation where the people are all sick and dying, "the people get up and come forth with happy faces." He is given visions of war, starvation, sickness, and weeping, but he goes forth in hope accompanied by the star, the sun, and the eagle. Before he was even fifteen years old, however, the assaults of the soldiers kept his people on the run until starvation eventually drove them to surrender. Black Elk frames his story as one about "a mighty vision given to a man too weak to use it; of a holy tree that should have flourished in a people's heart with flowers and singing birds, and now is withered." As an old man, Black Elk feels he has failed. He tells Neihardt, "You see now a pitiful old man who has done nothing, for the nation's hoop is broken and scattered. There is no center any longer, and the sacred tree is dead." In a postscript, Neihardt relates the story of a last journey Black Elk makes to pray to the Great Spirit, his Grandfather. He prays that some "little root of the sacred tree still lives" and that his people "may once more go back into the sacred hoop and find the good red road, the shielding tree." One act he still has the power to do in honor of his vision is to tell it to Neihardt so that it can be recorded and never lost.

The book is enfolded between the early vision of the young boy and the late prayers of the old man, and in between these moments, Black Elk unfolds the narrative of wars, betrayal, and removal that destroyed the hopes of his people. The treaty of 1868 had established the Great Sioux Reservation, which was essentially all of western South Dakota, including the Black Hills. The tribes resisted further carving away since the Black Hills were holy ground for them. In 1874 Lt. Col. George Armstrong Custer led an expedition that discovered gold in the Black Hills, and Custer publicized it through the eastern newspapers. Soon a flood of miners and the railroads wanted access to the region, which belonged by treaty to the Lakota. Black Elk was eleven when troubles intensified. In March 1876, soldiers attacked the village of Crazy Horse, killing women and children. Indians responded by fighting back. Black Elk's account of the attacks and celebrations of victories are lively and sometimes full of the fun of boys playing at being warriors. In June of the same year, Custer led the attack near the Little Bighorn River. Black Elk tells of the initial confusion at the surprise attack and of getting his first scalp, though he is only thirteen and not on the front line of fighting. He returned to his mother to show her his first scalp and watched the dust of the battle with her. His older friends from the Minneconjou and Uncpapas Sioux, Standing Bear and Iron Hawk, were in the thick of the battle. They add their firsthand accounts when excitement turns to violence, fear to courage. Readers who have seen one too many Custer movies will especially enjoy this version from the winning side. Later, the people gathered to eat and to sing the "kill songs" about "Long Hair" (Custer): You have "brought me many [horses], I thank you! / You make me laugh!" Black Elk summarizes his feelings, "I was not sorry at all. I was a happy boy. Those Wasichus had come to kill our mothers and fathers and us, and it was our country."

Unfortunately, the years after the victory at Little Bighorn were full of heartbreak and deprivation. Black Elk tells of the relentless pursuit by the soldiers and of the physical and psychological suffering during this period. Constantly moving to escape the soldiers meant that the band could not secure food sources or make warm tepees against the cold. It also meant that the vital community life with other bands was shattered. Increasingly, each small band was alone in its struggle. When Dull Knife and his Cheyenne people come to Black Elk's camp for help, they are starving and freezing. The Lakota can give them clothing, but there is little food to share because they are eating the ponies to keep themselves alive. Many perish in the extreme conditions, and Black Elk notes in particular that many babies died. The sense of being alone deepens when Dull Knife and his band depart for Soldiers' Town (Fort Robinson in the Pine Ridge area of Nebraska) to surrender.

For chiefs such as Dull Knife and Crazy Horse, Black Elk's cousin and chief, the burden of how best to protect their people weighed heavily on their hearts and minds. Crazy Horse had long been known for the oddities of some of his actions, but after Dull Knife leaves, the people observe that he increasingly goes off alone. He hardly ever eats and seems distant and strange in his behavior. The band manages to survive the sad and bitter winter of fighting the pursuing soldiers in snow and blizzard, and in the spring of 1877 Crazy Horse leads them to Soldiers' Town to surrender. The decision to surrender was a lonely and defeated one, bringing with it the loss of the Indian way of life and the humiliation of being treated as outlaws in their own land. At the end of the summer, on September 5, 1877, Crazy Horse is killed by the soldiers while in their custody. As the soldiers move against him, Crazy Horse cries out in Lakota, "Don't touch me! I am Crazy Horse!" This poignant last cry of pride and human dignity "went through all the people there like a big wind that strikes many trees all at once.'" Black Elk's eloquent metaphor was to become more true than figurative in the next decade.

By the early 1880s the bison herds had virtually all been killed, and many of the Native people were living in square houses (unlike the symbolic circle of their tepees) on reservations. "The nation's hoop was broken, and there was no center any longer for the flowering tree. The people were in despair," Black Elk tells us. His adventures in American cities and in Europe as part of Buffalo Bill's show deepen his alienation from white culture. From Chicago, Black Elk observes, "They would take everything from each other if they could, and so there were some who had more of everything than they could use, while crowds of people had nothing at all and maybe were starving. They had forgotten that the earth was their mother."

Although we think of putting Indians on display in a Wild West show as extreme cultural exploitation, Black Elk liked the show, and apparently Buffalo Bill was good to him. Certainly Queen Victoria was, in her royal way. She attended the show and was very impressed with the Native Americans in it. He remembers her telling them that they were "the best looking people" she knew and, "If you belonged to me, I would not let them take you around in a show like this." The Native Americans were given special seats in a parade honoring the Queen's Golden Jubilee, and she stopped in front of them and bowed. Black Elk liked "Grandmother England" and speculated, "Maybe if she had been our Grandmother, it would have been better for our people." And indeed, with the exception of some memorable episodes, Indian tribes in the Canadian provinces were not subject to the extreme violence that persisted for so many years in the United States.

When Black Elk returned to his people in 1889, their situation was worse than ever. A drought had killed the crops, and the whites were providing less than half the food they had promised. The treaty of 1889 took away another half of the land allotted them. The people were "penned up and could do nothing." Hungry and in despair, the people learned of a new sacred man, Frank Wilson (Wovoka), who was spreading an evangelical message that there was a way to restore the nations and the buffalo and drive the whites out. It was through the Ghost Dance. Black Elk is troubled by the stories, but when he goes to Wounded Knee to see for himself, he sees dancers using the same symbols he had seen in his vision as a boy. At the time, he was convinced of the power of the vision in the Ghost Dance: "I thought how in my vision everything was like old times and the tree was flowering, but when I came back the tree was dead. And I thought that if this world would do as the vision teaches, the tree could bloom here too." Later, he says that this was his "great mistake" and regrets following the vision of the Ghost Dance. Some readers see the visions in the Ghost Dance as influenced by stories of the coming of the messiah from Christianity. In *The Twilight of the Sioux* Neihardt overtly connects the vision behind the Ghost Dance to the Christian story of a messiah who is the son of God. Black Elk's account, as best we can judge, is far less explicit, and other accounts from Native Americans emphasize the vision's integral relationship to Indian religious practices.

As the Ghost Dance grew and spread, the soldiers were increasingly concerned that the dances might lead to renewed violence, and they sought to suppress it. The murder on the reservation of Sitting Bull by soldiers on December 15, 1890, created more anxiety on all sides and helped to set the stage for the massacre at Wounded Knee. Black Elk vividly describes the horrific scene with women and children dead and sometimes torn apart by cannons. The Indians fought with whatever weapons they had, but the soldiers had superior weapons and outnumbered them about five to one. At the close of the battle, snow began to fall and a blizzard covered the ground until "it was one long grave of butchered women and children and

Fig. 7. The "Medicine Man" was one of many bodies left frozen in the snow after the massacre at Wounded Knee, South Dakota. This photograph was taken January 3, 1891. RG 1227 PH 22-21. Courtesy of the Nebraska State Historical Society.

babies, who had never done any harm and were only trying to run away."

The next day, warriors attacked the Seventh Cavalry, and Black Elk's initial reluctance to kill had changed to a desire for revenge. He was wounded, but the fight continued until the arrival of the Fifth Cavalry turned the battle and Red Cloud had to make peace so that the women and children could survive. It was the end of the Indian wars in the United States.

The massacre at Wounded Knee burns in the history of American expansion and the fire of Manifest Destiny. Black Elk's story of the hope that spurred the Ghost Dance and the desire for revenge that drove the warriors to this last series of battles is an important account of the sorrowful end of those hopes to recapture their lost way of life on the Great Plains. No other chapter in American history except slavery is as protracted, misguided, and tragic as the destruction of the way of life of the Native Americans. Many Native Americans and a growing number of scholars view this history as no less than a policy of genocide. If not in official intent, in actions it resulted in the destruction of a way of life and the death of large percentages of the people. Embedded in the history of broken treaties and military attacks, as in the defense of slavery, was a resistance to recognizing Native Americans as human beings. Not until 1879 in the trial of Ponca chief Standing Bear, who argued, "I am a man," was there a legal ruling recognizing that an Indian is a person with individual rights under the law. The greatest value of *Black Elk Speaks* is that it brings to vivid life the common humanity that was often denied in a long history of war and removal. *Black Elk Speaks* is not just important for what it tells us about the Native American past; it serves as a fable for numerous other chapters in American history when other cultures and different people were in the way of some grand ambition of the nation.

The repression of Native culture did not end with the Indian wars, however. Life on the reservation was not just a confinement to land that was too limited to support the way of life of Plains tribes. In a misguided effort to teach Native Americans the ways of the white world, practices and policies were put in place that further destroyed traditional Indian cultures. The short stories of Zitkala-Ša (1876–1938) were among the first literary works to tell of life on the reservation and the separation of Indian children from their parents to attend Indian schools. Born on the Yankton Indian Reservation in South Dakota, Zitkala-Ša was a Dakota Sioux with the given name of Gertrude Simmons. When she was eight years old, she was taken to White's Manual Labor Institute in Wabash, Indiana, where she was a student from 1884 to 1887. She returned to White's from 1891 to 1895. A talented musician, she attended Earlham College on a scholarship and later played violin with the New England Conservatory of Music. In 1897 she began work at the Carlisle Indian Industrial School.

While away at school, Zitkala-Ša began writing down stories and legends of her people. From 1900 to 1902 she published stories in the *Atlantic Monthly* and *Harper's* that brought her much praise and attention from eastern literary circles. Her first book in 1901 was *Old Indian Legends*, and in 1921 she published *American Indian Stories*. In addition to her literary career, Zitkala-Ša collaborated with American composer William F. Hanson and wrote the libretto and songs for the opera *The Sun Dance*. Zitkala-Ša was also a well-known activist who served as editor of *American Indian Magazine* and founded the National Council of American Indians in 1926. She died in 1938, the same year the opera *The Sun Dance* opened in New York City. Her work was brought back for later generations of readers in 1985 when the University of Nebraska Press published new editions of *Old Indian Legends* and *American Indian Stories*. A collection of her miscellaneous writings was also published by the University of Nebraska Press in 2001. In 2003 her work was published in a Penguin Classic. Zitkala-Ša was also an activist with women's organizations, and her writings have become a valued part of the curriculum in both Native American and women's literature courses.

Zitkala-Ša's often-autobiographical stories are especially strong in their portrayal of the mother-daughter relationship, the trauma of the Indian schools, and the difficulty of life on the reservation without rights or access to justice. The mother-daughter stories remind us that during those harsh years of war and surrender to the agencies, children were growing up and family life continued. So many accounts of Native American history from 1870 to 1900 focus on the clashes of warriors with the military, the leadership of chiefs, or the broken treaties that it is easy to forget that women and children were there, too. Stories such as "My Mother," "The Beadwork," and "The Coffee-Making" charm us with their portraits of a young daughter of seven learning the art of sewing porcupine quills and beadwork from her mother or playing dress up and impersonating her mother's manners and voice. There is an atmosphere of love and security in her home, despite the occasional tears of her mother, who understands what the "paleface" has done. She tells her daughter, "We were once very happy. But the paleface has stolen our lands and driven us hither." The circle of family included close relationships with her mother (her father was dead), brother, aunts, and uncles, along with a variety of other elderly "grandfathers." "The Coffee-Making" tells of the day a guest came by while her mother was briefly away from the tepee. Aware of the customs of hospitality, the young girl at once "began to play the part of the generous hostess" by making some coffee for the guest—out of the cold coffee grounds still in the pot and muddy water from the Missouri River. Neither her mother nor the visiting warrior, who sipped the cup as courtesy demanded, said anything to embarrass her: "They treated my best judgment, poor as it was, with utmost respect. It was not till long years afterward that I learned how ridiculous a thing I had done."

The contrast between the childhood play in the embrace of caring family and the cold oppression of the Indian school is sharp and bitter. The purpose of these Indians schools was not just to educate but to "kill the Indian" in their students. The schools taught Christianity and the ways of the dominant, white culture, in the belief that acculturation was in the best interest of both the Indians and the whites. Gen. Richard Pratt (no relation!), who opened the first of these schools, believed in "immersing" the Indians in American civilization and "holding them there until they [we]re thoroughly soaked." The education begins with teaching the students English and punishing the children for using their native language. In her naïveté, the girl is eager to go; but her older brother, who had been away at school, and her mother are reluctant. The girl is excited about riding the "iron horse" and seeing a land where red apple trees grow. Her mother yields because she knows her daughter will need an education to survive in a white world. The "Land of the Red Apples" turns out to be as frightening as her mother and brother had feared. Dressed in clothes she finds too tight, her hair cut short in shingles, she can find no one to comfort her during the many "frights and punishments" of their lives. The sadness and cruelty of the "black" school years leaves "so long a shadow that it darkens the path of years that have since gone by." The misery of the children in the Indian school recalls the misery of the girls in Jane Eyre's infamous Lowood School in Charlotte Bronte's novel, but the school's purpose of eradicating the students' Native culture was even more pernicious. In "Retrospection" the young girl, now a young woman, realizes that in pursuit of "the white man's papers," she has given up her Native faith and her closeness to her mother. She questions "whether real life or long-lasting death" lies beneath what she calls a "semblance of civilization."

A third group of stories are concerned with the conditions on the reservation and the consequences of assimilating to the beliefs and ways of white culture. "A Trip Westward" tells of a visit the young woman, now a teacher herself, makes to her mother and brother. She finds the house in disrepair and her mother and brother without means to buy food. Her brother, who had been a government clerk on the reservation, was replaced by a white man in retaliation for trying to right a small injustice. Both mother and daughter are dispirited and without faith that "good or justice" will ever come from the paleface. In "A Soft-Hearted Sioux" a young man who was educated in the Indian schools has failed to grow into the man he was expected to be. His will to enter manhood in an Indian fashion has been eaten away by his absorption in "the soft heart of Christ." He needs to kill something in the hunt to provide food to his dying father, but he has been taught that killing is wrong. He is torn between traditions and can find no resolution.

One of the stories that best captures the corruption that flourished on the reservation is "The Widespread Enigma concerning Blue-Star Woman." Blue-Star is an orphan and has no relatives or papers with which to prove her membership in the Sioux tribe. Yet the application for her share of tribal land requires her to say who her parents were. She barely gets by on the generosity of friends who share food with her. One day, Blue-Star is visited by two Indian men who live off the graft of land deals. They offer her a deal to "fix it" in return for half the land and money she will receive in her share. Proudly they assert that they "fight crooks with crooks" and have "clever white lawyers" who work for them. Their "fix" for her share of land is just one of several schemes that victimize the innocent and the old. The ways of these men grow out of the people's dependence on a corrupt government run by petty bureaucrats. No longer taught the virtues of ancient Indian ways, the young men laugh, "We use crooks, and crooks use us in the skirmish over Indian lands." Zitkala-Ša's unsparing vision of the devastation that comes with the loss of Native culture is exacerbated by the bankruptcy of what is offered as the ways of white civilization. Her stories remind us that the only war against the Native American that ended at Wounded Knee was the one using live ammunition.

One of the things most threatened by the need to accommodate to the ways of the conqueror was the nomadic past of Plains Indians. With tribal culture under duress on the reservations and active efforts to shut down the use of Indian languages, the oral traditions that preserved legend and belief through many generations were in danger of being lost. Black Elk and Zitkala-Ša lived in the nineteenth century and learned their language and culture when the tribes were intact. Contemporary novelist N. Scott Momaday had to re-create in imagination the history of the Kiowa and the meaning of their traditions. *The Way to Rainy Mountain* combines three narrative voices: an ancestral voice, a historical commentary, and the author's personal voice.

Anthropologists say that the Kiowas had their ancient origins in North America in the Kootenay region of British Columbia about five thousand years ago, but Kiowa origin myth says they entered the world through a hollow log. Their oral history began a few hundred years ago in Montana and moved southward down the Great Plains, which they ruled until they surrendered and were moved to the Oklahoma reservation. Momaday says that there is "little material evidence" that the golden age of the Kiowas ever existed, "yet it is within the reach of memory still." The ancestral voices tell of the mythic exploits of people such as his grandfather, Mammedaty. Several stories focus on the special relationship Kiowa warriors had with their horses. Thinking of these stories, Momaday can "know the living motion of a horse and the sound of hooves" or "understand how it was that a man might be moved to preserve the bones of a horse—and another to steal them away." This poetic book is an exercise in imaginative memory in pursuit of a vanishing Native history. Momaday incorporates some of this text in his longer novel, *House Made of Dawn*, for which he was awarded the Pulitzer

Prize in 1969. With many awards for his literary work, he stands today as a notable contemporary American writer.

Nationally, the Native American population is growing today, and some reservations work well to sustain the economic stability of their members. A number of corrective rights and restitution decisions have recently come from the courts. Still, many of the reservations on the Great Plains are areas of desperate poverty, unemployment, and alcoholism. Though the plains states have the greatest number of reservations, with more collective acreage than elsewhere in the United States, Indians are largely invisible to most white residents. You will not see a reservation from the Interstate or the mall or the football stadium. That real estate is too valuable to be allotted to a tribe. Black Elk called Neihardt a Word Sender, and writers such as Zitkala-Ša and Momaday join him as powerful senders of words about the real lives and history of Great Plains Indians. The increasing literary reputation and readership of these writers are hopeful signs that the history of misunderstanding and mistreatment may eventually be superseded by a greater understanding of what was done to the indigenous people in the name of westward expansion.

CHAPTER THREE

Taking the Land in Rölvaag's Immigrant Saga

Our fathers wrung their bread from stocks and stones
And fenced their gardens with the Redmen's bones.
—Robert Lowell, "Children of Light"

In 1782, in *Letters from an American Farmer*, Hector St. John Crèvecoeur posed the question, "What is an American?" This question would riddle the new nation of somewhat *united* states throughout the nineteenth century. Defining what is an American was never simple, but the later influx of non-English speaking immigrants further complicated the issue. With the exception of Germans in Pennsylvania and the Dutch in New York, the colonies were primarily settled and clearly dominated by people with British roots. In the second half of the nineteenth century, the economic and political upheaval in Europe and the lure of undeveloped land in America attracted an increasing number of immigrants from northern, central, and eastern Europe. These later waves of immigration would redefine national identity; in the Great Plains the impact would be foundational.

The Great Plains were settled more than 250 years after Jamestown (1607) and Plymouth (1620). The mix of cultures on the plains was unlike that of either the Northeast or the South or of the moving frontier of the woods and mountains of states like Kentucky. The people who settled the plains came from

Scandinavia, Germany, Ireland, Russia, and eastern Europe. Later, its cities would attract Italians, Poles, eastern European Jews, southern blacks, and Latinos. Frederick Luebke's research on immigrants on the plains shows that the majority of settlers were foreign born. Largely untouched by slavery, the plains also attracted some African American homesteaders, and a few all-black communities were scattered across the plains. The story of one black settler in South Dakota is chronicled in Oscar Micheaux's novel *The Homesteader* (1917).

Unlike the first Irish immigrants, who were mainly Protestants from the North of Ireland, the midcentury Irish immigrants were Catholics from rural southern and western counties who were often fleeing the potato famine and land policies that displaced them. Many Scandinavian immigrants who came into the plains had initially settled in neighboring states like Minnesota, Iowa, and Wisconsin but moved west for more land. The majority were Lutherans. Unlike the first settlers in the colonies, the inhabitants of the nascent settlements of the plains often did not share a language, a religion, or an experience of any form of government by the people. For the territories of the Great Plains to become states in the nation, these settlers would have to learn how to become one people in a democracy.

Ole Edvart Rölvaag's classic trilogy of novels of the settlement on the plains, *Giants in the Earth* (1927), *Peder Victorious* (1929), and *Their Fathers' God* (1931), tells the stories of the Holm family and close friends, Norwegian immigrants, in the Dakota Territory from 1873 to 1896. Appropriately, this great American immigrant epic was originally written in Norwegian and published first in Norway. Rölvaag was himself an immigrant from a fishing village in Norway who came to South Dakota with no money and no English. Educated at St. Olaf College in Minnesota and the University of Oslo in Norway, he later

Fig. 8. Ole Edvart Rölvaag sitting in the backyard of his family home in Northfield, Minnesota. Courtesy of the Minnesota Historical Society.

joined the faculty at St. Olaf, where he published several novels about Norwegians in America and several textbooks about Norwegian language, literature, and culture.

Rölvaag's pioneering epic casts a cold eye on the emotional and physical costs of settling the prairie and displays a warm appreciation of the courage and cunning it took to succeed. Nothing is spared, but nothing is disparaged. Drawing on the memoirs of his wife's father and uncle who homesteaded in 1873 near Garretson, South Dakota, Rölvaag also interviewed many people who were immigrants to this area. His characters are drawn in great detail, with all their flaws and virtues, until they live on the page and stay with us indelibly in memory. Rölvaag shows us the psychological costs and changes that result from their pioneer life, but we also see the everyday details of that life. We know what they ate each night on the journey out, how

Fig. 9. Sod house with corn growing on the roof in Chapman, Custer County, near Walworth, Nebraska. Photographed in 1886 by Solomon D. Butcher. RG 2608 PH 0-1121. Courtesy of the Nebraska State Historical Society.

they lived until their sod house was made, where the furniture was placed, where they went for wood for the winter's heat, the odd comfort of having the animals under the same roof with them in the new sod house. We know how Per Hansa treated the infected arm of the Indian, how the wet laundry smelled drying in the house in winter, how much money they had, and what they bought at the store. We even know the special times Per Hansa made love to his wife. Rölvaag has a big theme for his novel, and these details make it vividly alive for the reader.

Giants in the Earth, the finest of the three novels, is much more than a wonderfully descriptive story of the hardships of the early settlers on the Great Plains. More than any novel I know, it illustrates *how* the immigrant becomes an American, and in doing that, it gives us one thoughtful and complex answer to Crèvecoeur's question. The main characters, Per

Hansa Holm and his wife Beret, react to the prairie environment and the conditions it imposes in diametrically opposite ways. Per Hansa embraces the emptiness of the land as pure opportunity. He is in love with this new life and the empty landscape. All he sees is the potential to succeed, to grow rich, to have a fine house, to be a leader in a community where there are no kings, in short, to be a free and independent man. His wife, Beret, is terrified of the emptiness, the open horizon, and the lack of everything she considers essential for civilized people. To her, the prairie threatens to destroy everything she values. To live here is to live like animals. Instead of reaching for what the new land might give in tribute to hard work, she devotes her energy to preserving everything she can of the old life in Norway. Together, the clash of these two personalities, with its consequences for the community and for the lives of their children, acts out both the bright and the dark sides of pioneer existence.

The little Dakota community of Spring Creek comes to recognize Per Hansa as the best farmer and the most accomplished leader. He wins these accolades because he is the archetypal capitalist entrepreneur: clever, hardworking, single-minded, and obsessed with succeeding. He is likable, generous, almost handsome, a good friend, and a loving husband and father. He also puts aside his wife's obvious terror and isolation, digs up the stakes of an Irish settler's land claim, and is possessed of the "indomitable conquering mood which seemed to give him the right of way wherever he went, whatever he did." Yet there is about him a kind of innocence that prevents him from seeing that something that succeeds could be wrong or have irremediable consequences. For him and others, the land was theirs for the taking, from the plains "to the Pacific Ocean." His excitement at the challenge of making a "kingdom" of his own in the new land and his love of the "beautiful" plains are catching. Readers may judge him, but they don't forget him. That his life does not end in a happy old age of enjoying the fruits of his labor seems tragic, if appropriate.

Per Hansa's willingness to push forward to take the land against all considerations becomes apparent on the first day he walks the acreage he hopes to claim. On "the spacious and beautiful" high point above the prairie, he finds Indian graves. His Norwegian friends, Tönseten and Hans Olsa, are shocked and subdued by the sight and know at once this is "rotten luck." Instead of honoring the gravesite and picking another quarter section, Per Hansa says, "We needn't shout the fact from the house-tops." "This kingdom is going to be *mine*!" he thinks, and "No ghost of a dead Indian [will] drive [me] away!" He later learns that an Indian trail to Nebraska runs through this spot, and when a band of Indians comes through, he fears that everyone will learn about the graves.

An even more worrisome episode occurs when Per Hansa destroys stakes that Irish settlers previously placed on the land that his friends, Hans Olsa and Tönseten, want to claim. Digging out the stakes to a legitimate claim would be criminal under U.S. law, but apparently destroying another's "landmarks" was also a heinous sin in Norwegian traditions. When Beret finds the stakes hidden in the stable, she thinks, "God forgive him, he was meddling with other folks' landmarks!" The narrator continues: "How often she had heard it said, both here and in the old country: a blacker sin than this a man could hardly commit against his fellows!" Per Hansa assures himself that the stakes cannot be legitimate (and apparently the Irish failed officially to file the claim). But Beret thinks they are sitting on another man's land, and the dishonorable behavior in her husband deepens her horror at the potential that life on the plains will make animals of them. When the Irish show up to claim the land, the conflict builds, and the Irish are challenged to find the stakes and to prove their case. After a few fisticuffs between the groups, the Irish withdraw but settle on other nearby sections. When Beret then hears the full story of her husband's deception, she is convinced that life on the prairie brings out the evil in them.

Per Hansa's entrepreneurial spirit supplants any foolish prejudice that others in the little community may hold against the Irish or the Indians. The Irish turn out to be good consumers of his potatoes. Talking with them over the sale, he decides that "the Irish [are] excellent folk," the "finest people in the world!" When an opportunity arises to secure furs from the Indians, he buys them at ten cents a fur, knowing that he can sell them in Minnesota for fifty cents. He makes four such trips and clears $140 after buying supplies for farm and home. Interestingly, he does not share word of this fur market with his two close friends, nor does he ever tell Beret of the risks he took or the dangers he encountered. Beret withholds her approval, and it is easy to judge Per Hansa's enthusiasm for making money as unprincipled. His commercial endeavors are, however, an ameliorating influence against prejudice and isolation among ethnic communities. In the nexus of trade, the Irish are "fine people" and the Indians are "just human beings." By creating an infant commercial network for the sale of goods, the settlers had to learn a common language, approach each other in courteous and friendly manners, and develop the codes of law and business that fairly governed their interactions. The presence of a commercial world, like the railroads, was as crucial a component of the successful permanent settlement of the Great Plains as was breaking the land and building sod huts. One of the great values of Rölvaag's work is the detailed illustration of how these economic connections developed across an "empty" land.

Fear and isolation were part of every settler's experience, but not everyone was equally adaptable to conditions on the

Great Plains. Rölvaag observes that "the strange spell of sadness which the unbroken solitude cast upon the minds of some" was a tribulation more to be dreaded than the attacks of "the Red Son of the Great Prairie." Many did not survive, many took their own lives, and many filled the asylums. "It is," he writes, "hard for the eye to wander from sky line to sky line, year in and year out, without finding a resting place!"

Women perhaps experienced the fear and isolation more sharply than men because they were less able to control their circumstances and less in contact with any world beyond the farm. Beret Holm is an extreme example of a woman who never wanted to homestead and never got over her terror of the vast unknown of the prairie. At times, the reader may find the excesses of her rigidity annoying; at other times, her fear is palpable and pathetic. Beret harbored a sense of guilt because she had given herself to her sexual love of Per Hansa before marriage and was pregnant when she married him against her parents' wishes. On the prairie where she said there is nothing to hide behind, her sins are magnified. She covers the window at night and hides in the chest from the "devil." At times, she loses touch with reality. Shortly before her son Peder is born, she is convinced she will die. Beret survives, and the birth of the baby pulls her back into life. When the child is baptized as Peder Victorious, however, she loses her senses again, thrashing about, foaming at the mouth, and shrieking hysterically, "This sin shall not happen! How can a man be *victorious* out here, where the evil one gets us all . . . are you stark mad?"

Her derangement deepens when a plague of grasshoppers descends on them. To her, the grasshoppers have been sent by the devil. She begins to hallucinate conversations with her dead mother, who she is convinced wants the baby with her in heaven. After the baptism, she tells her mother that the baby cannot come to her with a name the devil tricked Per Hansa into giving the child. In fear for his child's life, Per Hansa places the baby in the care of friends. The people around Beret also fear that she will harm her child and can see that she is lost in madness. On another occasion, she hears her sons use an "evil" word and loses control and whips the children with a willow switch, leaving long red welts on them. Though she had once been meticulously clean and neat, she becomes "shabby and unkempt," and Per Hansa sadly notes that she doesn't even "bother to wash herself" any longer. The grief and terror within the family is perhaps most explicit when one sobbing son asks his father if his mother has killed his little brother.

Beret's refuge against the emptiness and fear is in fanaticism. Only the rigidities of an extreme conservatism in Norwegian traditions and religious beliefs allow her to order the chaos of her mental world. Everything in her world becomes right or wrong, and she is the one who knows what is right. Even old friends can hardly tolerate her pious preaching at them about their wrongdoing. When people begin to modify the Norwegian form of names to accommodate American practice, she believes they are "discarding" "sacred things." She does not want anyone but Norwegians to be part of the community. When Per Hansa wants to help the Indian man whose arm is badly infected, she tries to dissuade him and says the Indians must take care of themselves. Her unwillingness to welcome the Irish is unrelenting.

Beret's fears are also a form of anger, and Per Hansa, who will not take her away, is often her target. Before her mental health broke, she was an affectionate and kindhearted woman deeply in love with her husband. Now she is harsh and judgmental, insisting that he do what she thinks must be done. The first time she says "Can't you shut up with that talk!" Per Hansa is shocked because "it had never happened . . . that she had shamed him before others." Before too long, the sexual relationship between them, which had been intense and cherished by both of them, ends. Per Hansa is in denial for many months about the depth of her terror and her deranged behavior. In his mind, she is the most kindhearted person he has ever known, but his own ambitions also stand in the way of understanding her plight. Only after the disastrous baptism does Per Hansa come to realize the toll the move to the prairie has taken on her. His hard work, his fear for his children's safety, and his worry and heartbreak about the change in his wife make Per Hansa an "old man long before his time." He tells the minister, "All my dreams have been crushed in misery [and] it's my own fault from beginning to end. . . . I reasoned like this, that where I found happiness others must find it as well."

The story of the Holm family continues into the next generation in *Peder Victorious*. After her husband's death, Beret's mental health stabilizes into a sane but rigid state of mind, and she becomes a very successful farmer. Around her the world she wants to preserve is breaking up. The children grow up wanting to be Americans and to speak English, but Beret wants them to speak Norwegian and practice the ways of the old country. She looks for a school that will teach them Norwegian ways. This scheme backfires on her, as the rule of the school prevents students from speaking Norwegian: "*This is an American school: in work and play alike we speak English only.*" Even her church splits apart as a group of more liberal Lutherans breaks away and starts its own church. The new church drops "Norwegian" out of its name. While some readers may find the narrative of the schism within the church a bit tedious, it is an important part of the story of settlement and assimilation. It is also an important part of the history of the Lutheran church in America, which remains divided between those who are more socially conservative and accept the Bible as the word of God and those who are more socially liberal and view the Bible as inspired by God. The incident of church schisms over liberal and conservative differences is similar to those that occur in all religions and into the present day, and Rölvaag's novel provides an understanding of how these divisions derive from both religious and cultural traditions and spill over into politics.

Peder, watching the strictness of the original church in punishing sinners and the ugly quarrels that arise as the church splits, decides that he wants nothing to do with any of it. In a daring moment that embarrasses her children and disturbs the congregation, Beret rises to the floor to speak, a thing no woman has ever done in the church. Her oldest son, the only one in the family who has a vote, votes against his mother's position. Soon he leaves home and heads to Montana. Beret's only daughter soon follows her brother. Peder, the youngest and nearest to Beret's heart, falls in love with—oh my God—an *Irish Catholic*! Yes, that little Irish group of homesteaders was there for the duration. Peder's best friend is Charley Doheny, and his best girl is Charley's sister, Susie. When Beret learns that Peder has been to the Dohenys' for lunch, she tells him, "You will have to find another playmate," because they are Irish and he is Norwegian. Sounding like his late father, Peder objects, "They are *people* just the same." His mother tells him, "They are of another kind. They have another faith, and that is dangerous." Her wisdom boils down to the aphorism "You can't mix wheat and potatoes in the same bin," but in a later and more vulgar metaphor, she thinks to herself, "Here they had mixed people as though they were of no more consequence than the swill they slopped together for their pigs."

The third novel, *Their Fathers' God*, takes us into the troubled marriage of Peder and Susie and into Peder's growing interest in politics during the famous 1896 presidential election between William Jennings Bryan and William McKinley. Peder is a gifted speaker with political ambitions, and though he likes the

Populists, he lines up to work for the Republicans because he is advised they will win. The Dohenys are all Democrats. Rölvaag describes the beginnings of local government and draws a vivid picture of this polarizing campaign with its inflated rhetoric and nasty personal attacks. Politics in the growing settlement turns out to be a reflection of the community's differences and breaks along class, ethnic, and religious lines.

As politics drives one more wedge between Peder and Susie, the marriage moves closer to destruction. Peder's distaste for religion makes him disrespectful of Susie's Catholic faith, and Susie, living with Peder in Beret's home, is surrounded by "Norskie" ways and misunderstandings about her culture and religion. At home, Beret runs things, and Susie feels she is "only in the way." Peder both hears it and "hear[s] it not," perhaps because he hopes to inherit his mother's farm and is unwilling to secure one for Susie and himself. The community gossips relentlessly about their "mixed marriage," and the priest declares marriages of this type are the "greatest bane, the greatest danger, confronting the Church." Peder's minister tells him he sold his soul "to the devil" by being married by a Catholic priest, and when the priest comes to call, Peder is openly rude to him.

With no support at home, in the community, or from the church, the young and immature couple has little chance of working things out. The conflict about religion leads Beret, fearing for the soul of the baby, to take it upon herself to arrange a secret Lutheran baptism. Susie, also fearing for the soul of her baby, bows to her family's insistence on a secret Catholic baptism. Susie is horrified when Beret confesses her "black" sin on her deathbed, and Peder is horrified when a political enemy tells an audience of Susie's secret baptism of baby Petie. This unbearable situation reaches its furious climax when Peder storms into their bedroom, rips Susie's crucifix off the wall and stomps on it, and then snatches up her rosary and grinds the beads under his heel. The future of the much-baptized little "Petie," also known as "Peder Emmanuel," also known as "Patrick St. Olaf," is left hanging as this first member of the third generation of Norwegian American settlers begins his young life among the irremediable conflict of families, cultures, religions, and ambitions.

Soon after Per Hansa's death, the minister told Beret that her "great sin" was her "discontent" "with God's special creatures, [her] fellow men." Because she insists on her harsh and fanatical judgments about everyone's rights and wrongs, she "experience[s] no real happiness." She comes to realize that had she behaved differently, "it might have been heaven between her and Per Hansa, instead [of] . . . hell." However, she is never able to change. Unfortunately, Peder and Susie act out another version of the same story. Peder cannot quit taunting Susie about what he considers the stupidity of her religion, and she increasingly withdraws into that religion as their disintegrating marriage drives her deeper into fear and sorrow. When Peder inherits Beret's farm, he has no family left to live on it with him.

Rölvaag's trilogy is an epic of the courage and endurance of settling the Great Plains, but it is also an epic of sorrow, loss, intolerance, fear, and ambition that brought both joy and despair. Though set in the Great Plains, it is a very American story. The answer to the question "What is an American?" is more than the qualities of self-reliance, ingenuity, love of liberty, and tolerance of others. The answer also arises out of the sheer terror of settling a land that was not a country yet, the distrust and cruelty that came with surviving among people one did not know or understand, and the assertion of religion and heritage that were inexorably changing in response to the demands of a new world unlike the one in which they originated. Rölvaag's capacity to combine great admiration for what was good and glorious with piercing insight and clarity about what was weak and mean gives these three novels their greatness. And they are not just about the pioneer days. Reading them, I remembered William Faulkner's famous line in *Requiem for a Nun*: "The past is never dead. It isn't even past." The roots of both the conservative and the radical politics of today, the self-reliance and distrust of outsiders, the small communities where everyone in need is a neighbor, and the never-ending prejudices against race and ethnicity, all arise out of the pioneer experience of building a new American culture. For all that the Great Plains ultimately gave to the new Americans, there was nothing there to greet them but endless grasslands, alien peoples, deadly weather, and the unrelenting fear for survival itself. Still, as Rölvaag tells us, "They threw themselves blindly into the Impossible, and accomplished the Unbelievable." That it cost so much suffering and tragedy is also critical to the story we tell ourselves of the past.

CHAPTER FOUR

Cather and the End of the "West"

We were the last romantics—chose for theme
Traditional sanctity and loveliness; . . .
But all is changed, that high horse riderless,
Though mounted in that saddle Homer rode
Where the swan drifts upon a darkening flood.
—W. B. Yeats, "Coole Park and Ballylee, 1931"

If Ole Rölvaag wrote the epic of the settlement of the prairie, Willa Cather wrote its elegy. Cather was born in Virginia in 1873, the first winter that the Holm family of *Giants in the Earth* was in the Dakota Territory. By the time Cather's family moved to Nebraska ten years later, Red Cloud was the county seat with a railroad line, and the university she would attend in Lincoln was almost fifteen years old. The raw epic of the first waves of settlers in an empty landscape was over, though her grandparents had memories of the earlier times. Of the twelve novels Cather wrote before her death in 1947, three of them read as a trilogy of life on the prairie from the 1880s into the early twentieth century. These novels combine farms and towns, wagons and railroads, new immigrant families living in sod huts and second and third generations living in brick and board homes in town. Neighbors even call from farm to farm on the telephone. *O Pioneers!*, *My Ántonia*, and *A Lost Lady* reflect the lives of people who have already stratified the

Fig. 10. Willa Cather (1873–1947). Photographed by Nickolas Murray. Signed by Cather and inscribed to "my friends in McCook." RG 1951 PH 0-771. Courtesy of the Nebraska State Historical Society.

class differences and societal manners that even the smallest organized communities begin to define. Cather laments "the very end of the road-making West" that has given way to a generation that dares nothing and wants nothing but to cut up the land for profit.

Cather's West is more mythic than historical and largely represented by Nebraska. This is nowhere more obvious than in the essay on Nebraska titled "The End of the First Cycle," which she wrote in 1923 as part of a series called These United States in *Nation* magazine. Nebraska, she says, "was a State before there were people in it." There were, of course, "people" in Nebraska before any white settlers arrived, but Cather may be thinking of Webster County, where Red Cloud is located. Nebraska was admitted to statehood in 1867, but Webster County opened up for homesteading in 1870. Elsewhere in the state, Bellevue was incorporated and had a newspaper by 1854, and Omaha was the capital from 1854 until Lincoln became the capital with statehood. Scarce as the population was per square mile, territorial Nebraska sent three regiments and more than three thousand men to fight in the Civil War between 1861 and 1865.

By 1923, when she wrote this essay, Cather had been living in cities of the East like Pittsburgh and New York for over twenty-five years. In her idealized description of Nebraska, even the winters are short, and the sod made "warm, comfortable, durable houses." Everett Dick's classic study, *The Sod House Frontier*, describes them as often uncomfortable, impossible to keep clean, and having leaky roofs because hard rain went through the sod. Cather's essay mainly divides the settlers into three groups: the political emigrants of the 1848 revolutions who left cultivated European backgrounds and built "large and very prosperous" communities; the economic emigrants seeking to make a living; and "the incomers from the South" who were "provincial and utterly without curiosity." The crop failures and financial depression of 1893–97 had "a salutary effect" because they "winnowed out the settlers with a purpose from the drifting malcontents who are ever seeking a land where man does not live by the sweat of his brow. The slack farmer moved on. Superfluous banks failed . . . the strongest stock survived."

That surviving "strongest stock" earned its rewards, according to Cather, and in the present she describes, "every farmer owns an automobile," the fields are all plowed by tractors, many of the farmhouses have bathrooms and electric lights, and "every farm house has a telephone." (Only 7.1 percent of Nebraska farms had electricity by 1935, twelve years after Cather's essay.) On Saturday nights the families all see a movie together, and on Monday morning the "crowds of happy looking children," wearing "cheerful, modern clothes," "elastic and vigorous in their movements," all head off to school." The dark side of this fine life is that "too much prosperity, too many moving pictures, too much gaudy fiction" have begun to corrupt these "showy" farmer boys and girls who want to look like movie stars. Cather writes, "We must face the fact that the splendid story of the pioneers is finished, and that no new story worthy to take its place has yet begun." The new generation, she claims, "hates to make anything, wants to live and die in an automobile . . . [and] want[s] to buy everything ready-made." Still, Cather closes the essay with the hope that "surely the materialism and showy extravagance" of the hour were "a passing phase."

These conflicts in values, both between different groups of immigrants and between succeeding generations, which Cather describes in the *Nation* essay, are progressively developed in *O Pioneers!*, *My Ántonia*, and *A Lost Lady*. In *O Pioneers!* Alexandra Bergson is made of the "strongest stock," and Marian Forrester in *The Lost Lady* married it. Marian Forrester, however, is then lost in the materialism of the little men who have corrupted what Cather thinks of as the pioneer virtues.

The further Cather moves away from characters who work at homesteading and running the farm, the more her characters become abstracts of what has gone wrong in the West. Although she talks about "the West," these novels focus on that section of the Great Plains she knew in and around Red Cloud. To maintain the romance of her West, Cather will ignore much of its history.

The time period that she portrays in these novels contained some of the most important historical events and figures in plains history, but she rarely mentions any of them. Although she graduated high school in 1890, the year of the Wounded Knee Massacre, there is no known mention of it in her published work or private correspondence, according to Professor Andrew Jewel of the Cather Digital Archive. The town in which she grew up was named after the famed Indian leader, Red Cloud; but Native Americans are only present in the novel in traces of trails and isolate graves. William Jennings Bryan had a home in Lincoln, and in 1900 Cather published an article titled "The Personal Side of William Jennings Bryan." In these novels, however, Bryan's famous Populist campaign is only casually mentioned to disparage one character's political interest. Many of her major characters are Czechs, and she is often praised for her use of immigrants as main characters. She describes little of actual Bohemian culture or the demographic profile common to immigrants like Mr. Shimerda. Cather sees the strength of characters like Ántonia and the beauty and initiative of the "hired girls," but the Bohemians in these three novels are typically seen by the community as poor, low-status people whose behavior is often questionable to the more prosperous farmers and townspeople.

If those first settlers on the plains momentarily escaped the mundane and mercenary world of towns and cities in the pure necessity of simply surviving, the familiar distinctions of money, education, and status soon asserted themselves. Small town environments also tended to stratify gender roles, since the expectations of the sexes were clear to all and enforced by the community. Cather herself had pushed the boundaries of gender roles by dressing like a man, calling herself William, and taking male roles in the plays in school. These three novels portray women who also challenge gender definitions in their battles to survive and often succeed in real if limited ways. Though they have gumption and intelligence to match their beauty and charm, all are hindered and judged in different ways by the rigidities of gender expectations for women. Unfortunately, they are also largely involved with men who are afraid to act on their love for them and who judge them, sometimes harshly and sometimes sentimentally. In their stories, Cather illustrates not just their fates but also the unraveling of her mythic version of westward expansion.

O Pioneers! (1913) was the first of these three novels of women on the prairie. Alexandra Bergson is the smart daughter of her dying Swedish father; and rather than leave his land in the care of his two dim-witted sons who would lose it, he puts Alexandra in charge. Like many immigrants from Europe, John Bergson has that "old-world belief that land, in itself, is desirable." Historically, land was the only reliable source of wealth in many European countries. Owning it represented not just having means, it also denoted social status and economic independence. For her father to lose the farm would have been to lose everything that motivated him to come to America. Alexandra understands the importance of land and will sacrifice her personal life to attain and keep it.

Ironically, Alexandra will bury herself in acquiring wealth through land and farming in order to see that her little brother, Emil, gets his education and a chance to be something in the larger world. She will prove much better at buying up land at cheap prices from families who have failed at farming than she will at creating the ideal life for Emil. Cather tells the reader that Alexandra's "mind was slow, truthful, steadfast," but that "she had not the least spark of cleverness." Initially, Alexandra seems cleverer by far than her nay-saying brothers; her nearly invisible mother, who thinks of nothing but making preserves and pickles; the Linstrum family, who are failing at farming; and an assortment of farmhands who are her eccentric and good-hearted helpers.

It is only when Alexandra's ambitions require that she understand other people if she is to succeed that we begin to see how blind she is to human nature, including her own. Like Per Hansa, she cannot imagine how differently other people might see things or that what she pursues might not bring about what she thought it would. She looks for opportunities to throw the handsome young Emil together with her exotically beautiful young Bohemian friend, Marie Tovesky, though Cather paints Marie as almost irresistible to men. Marie tries hard to be a good wife, but unfortunately she is married to a self-pitying bully with a jealous temper and a quick hand with a gun. How can this not turn out badly? How can Alexandra not see that her little brother is tormented by his passionate love for the married Marie? How can Alexandra make a sustaining life for herself while constantly denying any personal need of her own? These questions drive the plot of the novel and ultimately teach us what Cather meant when she said that Alexandra possessed no cleverness.

Both the strength of Alexandra's accomplishments and the failures of her imagination grow out of her struggle to extract the wealth of the land. "Her training had all been toward the end of making her proficient in what she had undertaken to do," Cather tells us. Her father had not been an especially good farmer, having worked in a shipyard in Sweden, and the prairie land required a different kind of farming than did European countries with their regular rainfall and more predictable climate. In the early years, just hanging on to the land required all one's energy and thought. John Bergson's mental time was spent counting the cattle over and over, calculating the weight his steers would gain by the spring. By the time Alexandra was twelve, she was following the markets and knew what it would cost to feed each steer. When she tries to explain why she wants Emil to go into the world and not be attached to the plow, she says, "We grow hard and heavy here. . . . Our minds get stiff." Cather describes her mind as "a white book, with clear writing about weather and beasts and growing things." For Alexandra, there is no place for much of anything else until the wealth she has built and the dreams she harbors for Emil die in the murder that ends his life.

From her teen years when she dressed in a man's coat and turned an "Amazonian fierceness" against even a passing male's admiration of her "shining mass of hair," Alexandra put aside the traditional expectations for a woman. Passionate love was beyond her imagination, and she never "guessed what was going on in Marie's mind" or Emil's. It was, Emil observed, her "blind side." With her friend, Carl Linstrum, Alexandra shares a sympathy of mind: "We've someway always felt alike about things . . . we've liked the same things and we've liked them together, without anybody else knowing." Although she tears up at the thought of how lonely she will be when Carl leaves, she thinks of this relationship as nothing except a good friendship. Carl, sensitive and emotional but feeling like "a fool" because he has not done anything to make her proud of him, insists he has never been of any real help to her.

In a well-known essay, critic Blanche Gelfant argues convincingly that many of Cather's main characters are afraid of sex and that sexual feelings are portrayed as destructive.

Except for an occasional recurring dream of being picked up and carried by a very strong person, Alexandra is oblivious to sexual feelings. Her platonic closeness to Carl through liking the same things together is all the intimacy she can imagine. Carl himself never seems to feel the pressure of desire, and only Marie and Emil seem to know anything about the power of a kiss. Carl always seems "to hold himself away from things, as if . . . afraid of being hurt," and he admits to Alexandra, "I am cowardly about things that remind me of myself." When Marie tries to stop Emil from expressing his love, she tells him, "We can never do nice things together any more. We shall have to behave like Mr. Linstrum."

Alexandra spends the next sixteen or so years rearing Emil as though he were her child and not her brother and acquiring more wealth. She is fair-minded and unflappable, protective of idiosyncratic friends whom the community would condemn, and generous with food to poor neighbors. Carl becomes an engraver but does not find the work satisfying and is on his way to Alaska to mine gold when he stops in Hanover (one of many names for Red Cloud) to visit Alexandra. Almost twenty years later, both of them are remarkably unchanged, but the world Alexandra has built is drifting toward disaster when Marie's husband murders his wife and Emil as they lie locked in each other's arms under the white mulberry tree, a symbol of forbidden love in Ovid and Shakespeare.

In a novel where the heroine and her lover, if we can call Carl that, just talk and write an occasional letter, it can be hard to move the plot along. Cather solves the plot problem by off-loading romantic love and sexual attraction onto the relationship between Emil and Marie. There the destructiveness of sex and passion can be played out without staining Alexandra and Carl. Even as a child, Marie is beautiful and "dark" with hair "like a brunette doll's." Alexandra remembers her looking like "some queer foreign kind of a doll," and Carl remembers that she had a toy of "a Turkish lady sitting on an ottoman and smoking a hookah." The Turkish lady was "lovely, and had a gold crescent on her turban."

No longer like a toy, the adult Marie is a sexual woman who falls in love and marries the first good-looking and aggressive man who wants her. For a costumed church supper in the French Church (Catholic), she dresses up like a gypsy fortune teller. A real life "Turkish" lady, she wears a "short" (for the times, of course) red skirt, a white bodice, "a yellow silk turban," and "long coral pendants" in her *pierced* ears. She is matched by Emil's equally colorful costume from Mexico. He appears as "a strikingly exotic figure in a tall Mexican hat, a silk sash, and a black velvet jacket, sewn with silver buttons." Two beautiful, exotic, erotic, and "foreign" young people embody the pleasures of sensuality in a society that is silent about sexuality and eschews extravagance of any kind.

The tragedy of this western Adonis and Aphrodite forces Alexandra to examine her share of the blame for their murders. She had loved Marie's bright spirit, and "it had never occurred to her that Emil's feeling might be different from her own." Even more than herself, she blames Marie. Marie's "happy, affectionate nature" had "brought destruction and sorrow to all who had loved her." Alexandra asks, "Was there, then, something wrong in being warm-hearted and impulsive like that?" Of course, it was Emil who pressed the kiss on Marie and Emil who had come uninvited to her place in search of yet one more goodbye. While Alexandra blames the lovely womanhood of Marie, Carl understands that the ruin was through no fault of Marie's, that "people come to" a woman full of life and love as "people go to a warm fire in winter." He tells Alexandra that when he was with them, even he felt "an acceleration of life." Visiting Marie's husband in prison, Alexandra intuitively recognizes her own prison, and a "disgust with life weigh[s] upon her heart."

Only Marie knew the guilt her husband, Frank Shabata, bore in the tragedy. Frank resents that his wife can be happy about anything that is outside of her relationship to him and that "the least thing in the world" could make her gay. He tries "to make her life ugly," and Marie recognizes that Frank wants a timid wife who cares about nothing in the world but her husband and that she is just the kind of wife he should not have. Frank wonders if he might have relented if he "could once have made Marie thoroughly unhappy" and then had the pleasure of raising her "from the dust." His grudge against her and the world is too important to him, however, so he tortures both of them, and his jealousy and bad temper only deepen his wife's disgust with him.

Frank is one of Cather's most masterfully done characters, and some of her best writing in the novel is of Frank's mind when he finds Marie and Emil together and kills them. Although Frank has taken his Winchester to investigate why Emil's horse is in his stable, he has no intention of doing anything with it: "He did not believe that he had any real grievance. But it gratified him to feel like a desperate man. He had got into the habit of seeing himself always in desperate straits." Frank's "unhappy temperament [is] like a cage" he cannot get out of. Cather tells us that Frank "would have been paralyzed with fright had he known that there was the slightest probability" of his doing what he actually does. When he fires the gun, he is filled with horror and terror. He acknowledges to himself that he has been doing Marie wrong, that he has been trying to break her spirit, to make her feel that life is ugly and unjust. As he runs to get away from the bloody horror of his bleeding wife, he can think only of how he wants to be comforted by her.

With her dreams shattered, Alexandra needs the companionship of Carl more than ever and is at last willing to leave the farm for a while and travel to Alaska with him. Ever the cautious and morally conventional woman, she reasons, "I think when friends marry, they are safe." Still, she again has her dream of strong arms carrying her, and she notes Carl's "lustrous black eyes, his whimsical smile," which no one would take as belonging "to a man of business." She is oppressed by a future of wearing the black clothes of mourning, reading another market analysis, and calculating the cost of feeding each steer during the winter.

Alexandra is a woman whose river of feeling runs so deep that she cannot drink from it. She is attracted to Marie because the flow of Marie's feelings bubbles over and nourishes everyone who loves warmth and beauty. Yet she blames those very traits for the destruction and woe in her life. All her adult years, Alexandra believed she made sacrifices to set Emil up in life, but in the end, Emil wanted nothing she could give him. Carl loves her and at last can ask her to marry him. Alexandra will never be "in love," but in her forties she at last may know a love that is more than just talk. Her story may remind us of Robert Frost's "The Oven Bird," in which a bird sings of petals fallen, days overcast, leaves grown old: "The question that he frames in all but words / Is what to make of a diminished thing."

In *My Ántonia* (1918), generally considered Cather's finest novel, many of the incipient class distinctions in *O Pioneers!* come to the fore and affect the lives of all the main characters. The women are constantly caught in gender and class constraints, but the men who sometimes most harshly enforce those constraints are damaged by them, too. The ethnic mix is more varied and includes Norwegians, Russian Germans, and Bohemians. Like Marie Tovesky, Ántonia Shimerda is a Bohemian girl whose eyes are "warm and full of light" and whose cheeks have "a glow of rich, dark color." Her "brown hair" is "curly and wild-looking." The novel's plot centers on her, but the novel's frame gives her story to a first-person narrator, Jim Burden, the man who creates *his* Ántonia in a memoir of his youth in Nebraska. Like Cather, the "author" of this memoir moves to Nebraska from "under the Blue Ridge" when he is ten. Ántonia's family is on the same train, and from that moment on, his youth on the plains is entwined with hers.

Jim Burden as narrator is a problem for critics and readers alike. First-person narrators may not be reliable, but since they control what we know about others in the story, they seem to speak with authority and lead us to identify with their point of view. If the narrative structure influences us to see Jim as credible and sympathetic, his parallels with Cather tend to make us think he represents her point of view. Many readers have seen him as a hero and accept his interpretation of his life and Ántonia's, but many others have not. Feminist critics have often seen him as self-involved, even narcissistic, a man who used women he found attractive but who could make no commitments to them. After critics began to read Cather through the lens of her lesbianism, the issue of Jim became even more complicated. Was he a manifestation of Cather's attraction to women like Ántonia and Marie, women of overt sexual appeal and warm, vital hearts? Was his timidity and failure to act on the love and sexual desire he felt an embodiment of the repression that Cather felt was required to subdue her lesbian feelings? How a reader interprets Jim will influence how the reader understands the characters and ultimately how one interprets the "meaning" of the novel.

Jim idealizes Ántonia in memory, as he does the Nebraska landscape that he was, in fact, eager to leave. Jim's real adult life has been full of disappointments. A lawyer for the railroads, Jim lives in New York in an apparently loveless marriage with no children. (There are two versions of the introduction, one of which paints a grimmer picture of his marriage than the other.) Given his "romantic disposition," in memory Ántonia has become an embodiment of "the country, the conditions, the whole adventure of [their] childhood." Jim's memories of childhood and youth reveal, however, some of the reasons that he failed to make anything out of that past that could lead to mature happiness in adulthood.

Ántonia's story, as we get it from Jim, is rather straightforward. Her family arrives in Webster County depleted of the resources they spent on the long journey and cheated by a conniving fellow Bohemian who sold them a sod cave that passes for a house. Her father, Mr. Shimerda, is from the city, a weaver by trade who plays violin and knows nothing of farming. Homesick and failing at farming, he has a withering soul and depressed mood that are preludes to his suicide. Ántonia takes pride in her ability to work as hard as a man. Later she takes a job in town as a "hired girl" for a respectable family. The lures of music and dancing, however, lead her to quarrel with the family and go to work in a hotel, a position considered inappropriate for a respectable young woman. Ántonia is misled by a young man who promises to marry her but leaves her pregnant in Denver. She returns home, eats humble pie, has her baby, and eventually marries a decent if not skillful farmer and has ten more happy and healthy children. She gets along with her husband, they make a decent living, she adores her children, and she retains into her forties the generosity of spirit and zest for life that she had as a girl.

The novel's primary interest in this rather ordinary story is in Jim's reactions to it. Ten-year-old Jim arrives from Virginia newly orphaned, feeling "the world [has been] left behind." The prairie makes him feel "erased, blotted out," and his grandmother's garden is the one place he can feel "entirely happy," "dissolved into something complete and great." At times, Jim finds the prairie beautiful and Ántonia lovely and friendly, but he is inhibited by his sense of class superiority and never overcomes his distaste for her "peasant" ways, which include her disturbing sexuality. His prosperous grandparents' home is "the only wooden house west of Black Hawk" (Red Cloud) for miles around. The Burden family is generous with food and neighborly assistance but looks askance at how the Shimerdas live like "badgers" in their cave and eat things the Burdens would not touch. Jim remembers being "horrified . . . at the sour, ashy-gray bread" Mrs. Shimerda gives her family to eat, the cooked cucumbers in milk, and the precious dried mushrooms that Mrs. Shimerda shares and that the Burdens throw out without a clue to what they are. What would the Burdens think today at the price people pay for a loaf of good eastern European sourdough bread, or the dozens of recipes online for Czech-style cucumbers in milk or yogurt or sour cream, or the variety of dried mushrooms in the produce section of the grocery store?

Four years older than Jim and with some hard experience behind her as an immigrant, Ántonia has a protective manner toward the orphaned boy. Jim resents this, however: "I hated a superior tone she sometimes took with me . . . I was a boy and she was a girl." There is, literally, a snake in this childhood Garden of Eden, a mythically big rattler whose "abominable muscularity . . . loathsome, fluid motion, [and] disgusting vitality" make Jim feel "sick." The boy manages to kill this "ancient Evil" and wins Ántonia's praise: "I never know you were so brave, Jim. . . . You is just like big mans." This scene is loaded with ironies. In reflection Jim knows that the snake was old without "much fight in him" and that his moment of being like "a big mans" is "a mock adventure." In her fear at the moment, Ántonia reverts to her native language when trying to warn Jim of the snake poised to strike right behind him. In his fear at the moment, Jim lashes out at her with an ethnic slur: "What did you jabber Bohunk for?" This scene of fear and disgust in the presence of the ancient symbol of sex and evil ends with Ántonia's riding home, "her bare legs swinging against the pony's sides," and Jim's feeling more disgusted and angry than like a brave, big man. It was, after all, himself whom Jim saved from the bite of this snake, in more ways than one.

The critical comments about the Shimerdas grow until Jim begins to find the family distasteful. Mrs. Shimerda is "a conceited, boastful old thing, and even misfortune [can]not humble her." Ántonia, now fifteen and doing a man's work in the field, has "a draught-horse neck" like one sees "among the peasant women in all old countries." Soon everything about the Shimerdas was "disagreeable" to Jim: "Ántonia ate so noisily now, like a man, and she yawned often at the table and kept stretching her arms over her head as if they ached." She is burned brown by the sun—not fashionable at the time—and doing "chores a girl ought not to do." Even the farmhands joke about her in "a nasty way." The distance between the two families grows until fisticuffs break out and harsh and insulting words are exchanged. Ántonia is aware of Jim's disappointment and his grandmother's disapproval of her ways, but she explains to him how the divide between their statuses matters: "If I live here, like you, that is different. Things will be easy for you. But they will be hard for us."

Although we see and hear too little of Jim's grandfather, he is the one character who seems not to participate in the derogatory class and ethnic attitudes. Even after the fight that ends in harsh words, grandfather maintains a friendly relationship with the Shimerdas and eventually brings about a reconciliation of neighborly feelings. Although his kindness and acceptance of the Shimerdas gets only a few paragraphs in a long novel, it stands out in contrast to how quickly pejorative attitudes against "foreigners" surface any time recent immigrants from elsewhere differ from the values and habits of the more established generations.

Perhaps the most interesting and original sections of the novel are "The Hired Girls" and "Lena Lingard." Lena and Ántonia are among a handful of exceptionally attractive and lively young immigrant women who go to Black Hawk to work. All of them do so to earn money for their farm families and help the younger children get an education. They are the "hired girls" who work as domestics in private homes or as seamstresses and clerks in businesses such as the Boys' Home Hotel. The townspeople are quite aware of how pretty they are and consider them a "menace to the social order." The young men, even from the best families, are attracted to these "fine, well set-up country girls," but these girls are only for fun and dalliance, not for marriage. Jim, whose family has moved to town, too, sees them as "almost a race apart" from the town girls, who did not do heavy farmwork. The girls from the country had bodies that moved inside their clothes and danced the night away. Jim understands that the attitudes of the townspeople are "very stupid," but he also reasons that there was no cause for real worry, because "the respect for respectability [is] stronger than any desire in Black Hawk youth," himself included. He admits, "Disapprobation hurt me, even that of people whom I did not admire."

Disappointed in Ántonia, Jim is infatuated with Lena Lingard, who is working in Lincoln, where Jim is enrolled in college. A Norwegian, Lena is dazzlingly beautiful and feminine, dresses exceptionally well on her small budget, and is kind and courteous to everyone, including the many men who are half in love with her. Lena has even learned not to sound "impulsive and foreign in her speech" as Ántonia does. Her skin does not burn or tan under the hot sun, and her "whiteness" "somehow ma[kes] her seem more undressed than other girls who went scantily clad." Lena is perhaps an erotic displacement of the unacceptable feelings Jim has for Ántonia. Lena is safe: she does not want a husband or children, she demands nothing from Jim, she is never an embarrassment, and she is not passionate. Jim can enjoy the sexual ambience around Lena without commitment or cost.

When Jim returns to Black Hawk before going on to Harvard to complete his degree, he hears at once the pitying gossip about "poor Ántonia" and her baby. He cannot "forgive her for becoming an object of pity" or for having "thrown herself away on such a cheap sort of fellow." Ántonia's situation ends her youth and Jim's childhood. In a last visit, Jim and Ántonia say their farewells. Now that her disgrace has made her safely beyond all boundaries that a respectable young man like Jim can violate, he tells her, "I'd have liked to have you for a sweetheart, or a wife, or my mother or my sister—anything that a woman can be to a man." As he leaves her and the countryside, he wishes that he "could be a little boy again, and that [his] way could end there." When Jim returns twenty years later, he finds his boyhood again in Ántonia's "boys," whom he plans to visit each year and take on hunting and fishing outings, walking the prairies again, and idealizing Ántonia as one with whom he possesses "the precious, the incommunicable past."

Whether Jim is at all honest with himself or deluding himself with a romantic nostalgia for a world and a woman he left behind, whether his memoir is about Ántonia or a self-justifying story of his own childhood, the past is clearly past in this case. Now at a distance, he must mythologize the past to make it precious, to place the people and places outside time. From being a rough-hewn Eve in the Garden of the West, the matronly Ántonia has become the earth mother out of whose body the world will grow and be nourished. She is mother, sister, sweetheart, wife, friend—all the things a woman can be in Jim's imagination. Or not. Ántonia lives surrounded by a boisterous, happy, and loving family in a modest home on a small but sustaining farm. Jim, his memories now solidified in words, will still ride the trains back and forth across the country, returning to the loveless home in New York and looking forward to a vacation each summer when he can visit the woman he never tried to win and play with the children she had with someone else.

The old road of their childhood together on the open prairie has almost disappeared, but in his imagination Jim can still hear "the rumblings of the wagons in the dark" along "the road of Destiny," which, Jim says, "predetermined for us all we [could] ever be." If all is predetermined, he has indeed come home to himself, since nothing could have been otherwise, but the question of who exactly is at home remains. Despite the soaring rhetoric, the novel's mood of sadness lingers for a time and a place that can only live in the selective distortions of memory.

The elegiac mood of *My Ántonia* turns into bitter disappointment at what is spoiled and corrupted in *A Lost Lady* (1923). Again we have a beautiful, charming, and sexually alive woman, Marian Forrester, as seen through the eyes of Niel Herbert, a sensitive and immature young man with a romanticizing and moralizing sensibility. By virtue of living with his uncle who is a judge in Sweet Water (another version of Red Cloud), Niel is part of the "grey" town's upper crust, and Marian is the wife of the leading wealthy older man who helped build the railroads across the West. Marian has blue-black hair and is even attractive in "*dishabille*," and she "kn[ows] it." With her stylish clothes and pendant earrings—she has them in coral, garnet, and diamonds, all of which dangle seductively along her "pale triangular cheeks"—she belongs to a different class from the "common people." For Niel and much of the rest of the community, she embodies a perfect lady until her husband loses his money and is weakened by strokes.

Unlike *My Ántonia*, *A Lost Lady* is told by an omniscient narrator, but everything we learn about the characters reflects Niel's knowledge of them. Yet Niel's understanding of the dynamics revealed in this story is as flawed as is Jim Burden's. Niel is a rather callow young man in his late teens who is disappointed that the older woman he idealizes turns out to be less perfect than he wants to believe. His view of Marian Forrester repeats the pattern we saw in *My Ántonia* of a young man preoccupied with a woman's sexuality without recognizing how his own attraction influences his interpretation. Readers need to question Niel's account of Mrs. Forrester and to ask if the omniscient narrator is also Cather's voice or a narrative disguise to keep us from hearing Cather's voice.

From the first page, we are told that this story is about "two distinct social strata in the prairie States: the homesteaders and hand-workers who were there to make a living, and the bankers and gentlemen ranchers who came from the Atlantic seaboard to invest money and to 'develop our great West.'" But the two social strata are not that distinct in the actual divisions and social mobility of a young country. Mr. Forrester belongs to the aristocracy of those who built and run the railroad. He is neither a homesteader nor a handworker there to make a living, nor is he exactly a banker or gentleman rancher there to invest money. Niel's status is undeservedly in the upper social strata because he has so far done nothing but live with his uncle who is a judge. What is clearer is who belongs in the unworthy lower strata.

Although Mrs. Forrester will first be brought low in the eyes of Niel through a sexual affair, more importantly she undermines the "two distinct social strata" by spreading her charm to the coarse and common men and boys who live around her. A crude and cruel local boy named Ivy Peters will eventually buy up the Forrester house and land and make free with Mrs. Forrester herself. Long before he has the ability to own Mrs. Forrester's world, Ivy asserts, "I'm just as good as she is." With his dry red skin, small eyes, no eyelashes, and hard face, Ivy is described as looking like someone who stepped out of *Deliverance*. We know there is no hope for this fellow when he catches a woodpecker, slits its eyes, and then enjoys its panicked blind flight.

For Niel, Mrs. Forrester's fall is also a metaphor for how the old West gives way to the rise of a meretricious class that wants nothing from the West except to exploit it. As a wife, she represented the grace and beauty that heroic and successful men like her husband could own. Corrupt men like Ivy Peters and Mrs. Forrester's lover, Frank Ellinger, represent the men who came after Mr. Forrester's generation. Mrs. Forrester falls off the pedestal when she consorts with men like them, and Niel holds it against her "that she was not willing to immolate herself . . . and die with the pioneer period to which she belonged." He is brutal in his condemnation of her, quoting Shakespeare: "Lilies that fester smell far worse than weeds."

The narrator tells us that "it was as Mr. Forrester's wife that she most interested" Niel, and "it was in her relation to her husband that he most admired her." Niel's fascination with every piece of clothing and jewelry that Mrs. Forrester has worn, every sexually nuanced interaction she has had, suggests something more than his admiration for her wifely virtues. He wants to ask her what she does with her exquisiteness when she is in bed with a man like Frank Ellinger. In comments that recall Alexandra's assignment of blame to Marie, Niel muses, "Beautiful women . . . was their brilliancy always fed by something coarse and concealed? Was that their secret?" It never occurs to him that the "secret" that is concealed might be his own guilty erotic fascination with her.

In his mythic vision, Niel believes "the Old West" was "settled by dreamers, a courteous brotherhood, strong in attack but weak in defence, who could conquer but could not hold" and that men like Ivy will "destroy and cut up into profitable bits" all that the "great-hearted adventurers" had won. In Niel's mind, Ivy's generation is "trained to petty economies," such as his buying land cheap from the Indians, unlike Mr. Forrester's generation, who brought corporate economies like the railroads. Aside from the government, the railroad companies possessed more land in the West than any other entity, and they "cut up into profitable bits" the land and sold it. The anticipated commerce that the railroads expected to develop out of the West was also a driving force in federal efforts to eradicate the menace of the Native Americans that lived there.

Niel wants to "save" Mrs. Forrester, but at times, it seems that she would like to save him. Niel recognizes that even before Mrs. Forrester's fall, "she couldn't help being interested in people, even very commonplace people," and that she always treated even the servants and the poorest lad in the neighborhood "like a human being." To Niel, her indiscriminate interest in people below her socially is a betrayal of "an aesthetic ideal" she represented to him. Mrs. Forrester, however, sees that the boys think of Niel as a snob, and she advises him, "You mustn't be so stiff, so—so superior! It isn't becoming, at your age." Niel, however, has no interest in conquering his feelings of superiority or his view that Mrs. Forrester is "ruined" by her affair with Frank and her interest in the local rubes who are incapable of appreciating the quality of the china and silver on her table.

Niel cannot fully appreciate the terror Mrs. Forrester feels as a woman alone in a world run by men when she is widowed with almost no resources. She does not know what will become of her and is not ready "to immolate herself" and die just because her husband did. She still feels inside herself "such a power to live," she tells him, but doing so will involve dealing with men like Ivy and the realities of money. She will need to use all the charm, beauty, and made-over dresses she possesses to influence her future. She has the determination, the cleverness, and the beauty of a Scarlett O'Hara, but unlike the haughty Scarlett, Mrs. Forrester is a gracious woman to all kinds of people.

Cather created some of the most memorable women characters in American fiction in the first half of the twentieth century. Alexandra, Ántonia, Lena, and Mrs. Forrester are spirited heroines who survive the troubles in their lives and find some satisfaction and success. Even the most mean-spirited and self-pitying of the men are vividly alive on the page—men like Frank Shabata, Ivy Peters, or Alexandra's dumb brothers. Carl Linstrum, Jim Burden, and Niel Herbert are more problematic, and since the perspective in two of the novels is so much given to them, readers are forced to read through and around them to see what might be there that these self-involved young men do not see. Carl's confidence is undermined by his failure to make either art or money sufficient to merit Alexandra until tragedy brings her low. Jim suspects at heart that he is the mock hero of his nostalgic childhood story, and Niel cannot sustain the image of class superiority and aestheticism on which he has built his sense of self-importance.

Cather's novels of the generations that followed the first settlers have been important to many people who feel that their lives and histories are in some ways reflected in them. No doubt they are, but saying just *what* is reflected is the hard part. Cather's romantic West is without the troubled history that accompanied westward expansion, either in its justifications for destroying Native Americans or in the opportunism that exploited resources and the dreams of the settlers who believed that free land would bring security for their families.

The mythic West will always disappoint when history offers up its harsh corrections. Cather shows us the failures of the Shimerdas and Linstrums, the meanness in men like Ivy, the limits of wealth and land in the life of Alexandra, the complacency of small towns. None of these things, however, obscure the strength of Ántonia, the drive of Alexandra, the cleverness of Mrs. Forrester. Willa Cather left the plains for life in eastern cities but imaginatively turned back to it in the fiction that made her a renowned American writer. It is important, but not easy, to see in her novels of the West what was once there that is lost, as well as what was never there at all.

CHAPTER FIVE

Dissent and the Great Depression

> They lowered their heads and shut their eyes against the flaying
> sand and let the wind blow them to shelter or to the deaths of
> whatever
> worlds they kept inside their heads while the desert's dry convulsion
> annihilated the world outside.
> —Lois Phillips Hudson, *The Bones of Plenty*

People from across the United States and Europe made the journey to the Great Plains with the dream of being land owners and successful farmers. The dream was hard to make into a reality. The quixotic weather had numerous ways to kill a crop, but what could really push a farmer under were bank loans and market prices. Many a farmer who could eek out enough to feed the family when the crop was ruined could not find the cash to meet the mortgage payment or the loan taken out for improvements when times were good. More than one drought and depression had occurred before the "Great" one hit in the 1930s, but none recorded earlier had lasted so long or resulted in changes so profound that they altered the structure of agriculture and the ways that government attempted to deal with it. And no event in plains history except the saga of the early settlers and Indian wars would inspire literary and cultural representations of such passion, pathos, and popularity as the Great Depression.

The Dust Bowl, a label coined in the media to describe conditions in Oklahoma, Texas, and Kansas, generated a popular culture of songs and singers, films, photography, and literature. Between the songs of Woody Guthrie and the popularity of John Steinbeck's *The Grapes of Wrath*, the "Okies" became the signature media image of the plight of Dust Bowl farmers. A drought that lasted about a decade and the massive erosion of the top soil turned depression into tragedy for thousands of farm families who lost everything they had, often including the land their parents and grandparents had originally homesteaded. The cultural representations of the Depression on the plains almost always connected the farmer's desperation with dissident movements. Long before the crash in 1929, the farm economy was in trouble. Farmers did not benefit from the generally good times of the 1920s because surplus production resulted in falling prices. The faltering of the national economy after 1929 deepened the decline of farm prices, increased the number of foreclosures, and gave a new urgency to protest efforts.

Farm movements reflecting economic trouble on the plains began surfacing in the latter part of the nineteenth century. The Populist movement had wide influence throughout the Great Plains as well as in the South, but after endorsing William Jennings Bryan in 1896, its distinct identity was largely submerged in the Democratic Party. In 1915 the Nonpartisan League (NPL) emerged. The NPL would come to control the North Dakota state legislature and implement several state-owned institutions, such as the state bank or grain elevator. These movements and others that emerged in the 1920s and 1930s, such as the Farmers' Union, the Farmers' Holiday Association, and the cooperatives, addressed the anger and distrust that many American farmers felt toward a capitalist economy controlled by banks and markets outside the region.

Steinbeck, who was a Californian, had a very limited experience of the Great Plains, but no book about the Depression is more widely known than *The Grapes of Wrath*. It was the best-selling novel of 1939 and then became the best-selling film of 1940, starring Henry Fonda. For better and for worse, the story of the Joad family from Oklahoma, plowed out by the banks, fleeing the dust and hunger with all their belongings on a rickety old truck bound for California, is the iconic image of plains farmers displaced by the Dust Bowl. The Joads were Okies, the simple but honest folk who were the generic descendants of the original yeomen farmers on whom America had relied since the first shots fired on the British at Concord in 1775. As Ma Joad tells her son Tom, "Why, we're the people—we go on."

Steinbeck began writing about the Okie migrant workers in 1936 in the *San Francisco News*. Eventually he published these articles in a pamphlet, *Their Blood Is Strong* (1938), about the living conditions of the migrant workers. Like many writers who leaned to the left politically in the 1930s, Steinbeck hoped that by organizing, the migrant workers could successfully demand an improvement in their wages and living conditions. He traveled around the migrant camps in Salinas and Bakersfield, but in 1937 he went to Oklahoma and traveled back to California with a family of Okies. Steinbeck was moved by the tragedy of families starving and living in Hoovervilles, and he also conceptualized their plight as the betrayal of the agrarian promise that had driven so much of American development. He saw that the new industrialized agriculture was making the labor of small farmers and tenants an anachronism and that a long and important era of small independent farmers in America was coming to a close.

Although Steinbeck thought all migrant workers lived in terrible conditions, he was less sympathetic to the "foreign" migrants than to the white Okies, whom he considered

"American people" born to the "frontier tradition." He believed that their heritage of proud independence meant that they would help organize the union. Walter J. Stein's *California and the Dust Bowl Migration* argues, however, that the impact of the Okies was "to impede unionization and lower the already intolerable standards of living of agricultural labor," in part because "their ideologies conformed, not conflicted, with the ideologies of their exploiters." Despite Tom Joad's simple eloquence of what the people could do if they worked together, the Okies thought of themselves as the people who were meant to own the land and not as the working class.

The opening chapters of *The Grapes of Wrath* bring together the dust storms, the drought, and the banks to show the reader just how complex and interrelated these elements of the drama are. Steinbeck paints a powerful picture of how the rains stopped and the land dried out. If we put his prose into lines like poetry, we can see the poetic quality of his description:

> To the red country
> and part of the gray country . . .
> the surface of the earth crusted,
> a thin hard crust,
> and as the sky became pale,
> so the earth became pale,
> pink in the red country
> and white in the gray country.

The dust is so pervasive that even the air is "an emulsion of dust and air" that blocks out sunlight by day, starlight by night, and silences the world with its soft, black pollen.

The monster that is taking the Joads' farm is not, however, the dust. This generic story is about borrowing money from the bank, whether in bad years to hang on or in good years to expand, and not being able to pay it back. The tenant farmers and sharecroppers did not qualify for government farm-support programs since they did not own the land. Steinbeck's tenant farmers protest that "being born on [the land], working it, [and] dying on it ... makes ownership, not a paper with numbers on it." When they consider trying to remain and fight the bank, the sheriff tells them, "You'll be stealing it if you try to stay, you'll be murderers if you kill to stay." Like an army of giant mechanical insects, the tractors grate across the farm land, not plowing but "raping methodically" to suit the corporate interests. When the farmers challenge the driver to think of the people he is sending into starvation, the driver thinks only of the three dollars a day that will feed his family. Times are changing, he tells them: "Can't make a living on the land unless you've got two, five, ten thousand acres and a tractor. Crop land isn't for little guys like us any more." Unlike the old days when there were Indians to shoot to keep the land, these farmers can't shoot the bank that gets its directive from "the East." Even the goggled tractor driver raping the land is just one more farmer who has lost his land and was lucky enough to get the job.

Steinbeck is less interested in the hardscrabble farm life than in a mythic story of the yeoman farmer and how a man like Tom Joad will emerge to unify "the people." Tom Joad is a mix of American transcendentalism with a dash of Communist rhetoric. He learns from Preacher Casy that "a fella ain't no good alone." Casy's belief that men's souls are all only a piece of a big one translates Emerson's over-soul in service to organizing the people into something like a union, though Steinbeck is less precise about what that means than he is in his earlier novel, *In Dubious Battle* (1936), about Party organizers of a strike by fruit pickers. Tom's farewell to Ma as he goes forward to lead the migrants against the evil forces is an everyman's version of Walt Whitman's "Song of Myself":

Fig. 11. Dust storm with farmhouse in North Dakota in the 1930s. Courtesy of the Institute for Regional Studies, North Dakota State University, Fargo (2039.17.1).

I'll be ever'where—wherever you look. Wherever they's a fight so hungry people can eat, I'll be there. Wherever they's a cop beatin' up a guy, I'll be there. . . . I'll be in the way guys yell when they're mad an'—I'll be in the way kids laugh when they're hungry and they know supper's ready. An' when our folks eat the stuff they raise an' live in the houses they build—why, I'll be there.

Steinbeck's novel gets its power from the harsh details of migrant living and the theme of betrayal of nineteenth-century romanticism about the promise of American democracy. As a literary representation of the impact of the Dust Bowl or the Depression on the Great Plains, it leaves much unsaid. The

Okies of *The Grapes of Wrath* are tenant cotton farmers or sharecroppers in a section of Oklahoma, but wheat farmers in Kansas, Nebraska, the Dakotas, and the Prairie Provinces were much more typical. Some historians have argued that there were two other dust bowl areas, one in the northern plains states and another in the Prairie Provinces, and the literature from these areas tends to confirm that conditions there were equally bad. Other authors, less well known than Steinbeck, provide us a more nuanced portrait of conditions elsewhere and the varied responses to it.

The Bones of Plenty (1962) by Lois Phillips Hudson takes us to the wheat fields of North Dakota and the struggles of the Custer family. This highly praised novel, noted for the accuracy of its research, shows us what farm families went through during the years they worked to stay on the land. *The Bones of Plenty* and Hudson's collection of short stories, *Reapers of the Dust: A Prairie Chronicle* (1957), draw their inspiration from the experiences of Hudson's family. She was born in Jamestown, North Dakota, in 1927 to a family that also struggled during the Great Depression. The family eventually gave up the farm and left Cleveland, North Dakota, for Washington, where they were for a while migrant workers. Hudson returned to teach at North Dakota State University from 1967 to 1969 and then taught at the University of Washington from 1969 to 1992. She died on December 24, 2010.

The Bones of Plenty is built around the fates of two interwoven families of North Dakota wheat farmers. George Armstrong Custer (who is proud to be named after the famous one); his wife, Rachel; and their two daughters are tenant farmers. His father-in-law, Will Shepard; Will's wife, Rose; and their grown son, Stuart, live nearby and own their farm. As George is always grudgingly explaining, Will and Rose got their farm during the first decade of the century and made good money during the World War I years, when the demand for wheat was high. George hates his wife's parents because they are "lucky hypocrites that just happened to be born at the right time." George and his generation got their land in the mid-1920s when crop prices were falling. The story takes place from February 17, 1933, through May 25, 1934. Each chapter is identified by the exact day on which the action occurs.

Those of us who think that knowing exactly when and where things happen is important to understanding them will appreciate knowing that this story is in 1933–34, not 1931 or 1936 or something as vague as "the 1930s." In these fifteen months, the Custers financially go under and yield the farm to the landlord. The modestly more comfortable Shepards face their own decline through Will's death from cancer, medical debts, and some ruinous decisions by their son, who marries a young woman his widowed mother loathes having in the house. Hudson takes the reader through the stories of these two families step-by-step with wonderful detail as life overwhelms them. The rich detail makes the historical moment come to life, but her equally powerful portraits of the characters in the drama lift the novel into the ranks of lasting literary value.

The novel opens with the closing of the local bank of Eureka (based on Cleveland, North Dakota). Hudson quickly sets up two very different experiences and attitudes about the bank's failure. Will Shepherd, a decent man who always treats people in a polite and friendly manner, goes to the bank to cash a ten-dollar check and comes away, at the insistence of the banker, with a withdrawal of the entire contents of his account, $2,867. The banker, Harry Goodman, is planning to close the bank and abscond with enough money ($2,000) for a fresh start somewhere else. Will has always been a friend to Goodman in a town where many others call him "the little Jew banker." The severe deflation of property values has left the Eureka Bank with too many worthless mortgages to avoid collapse. The other experience belongs to George Custer, who has $250 in the bank to buy seed for the spring planting. George, who is virulently anti-Semitic, loses his money, and his bigoted epithets about Harry do the linguistic violence he wishes he could do physically.

In today's parlance, George has a raging anger-management problem. He does not intend to be a mean and harsh man, and he loves his daughters and his wife. George is dominated by his sense of being victimized by an unfair world. Lacking financial control of his land or equity for his hard work, George responds with harsh anger to everyone with any real or imagined power over him. Even President Franklin Roosevelt makes him furious by saying, "The only thing we have to fear is fear itself." George lays out the problem differently:

> The issue was that a rich man was telling them all not to worry even if they had just lost their last red cent to a little Jew banker, a rich man who couldn't possibly imagine what it was like to work sixteen hours a day for six months of the year and to sit in a dark house smothering in snow for the other six months, wondering where the money for coal was going to come from.

Even FDR's "fireside chats" anger George, who thinks "chat" is "an effete word" and a fireplace is "an expensive luxury" that only sucks the heat up the chimney.

One man George cannot beat is James T. Vick, who owns the land George rents. Vick is a store owner in Jamestown, some thirty miles from the farm, but he wants to tell George what to plant and on how many acres. Whereas George's decisions about his crops are based on his farming expertise, which is considerable, Vick's opinion is based on what the market advisers predict will bring the biggest profits. As the landlord, Vick's rule is simple: George can "obey or lose his lease." Twice in the novel, George tries to negotiate a deal with Vick that he thinks he can make work for both of them, and each effort ends in explosive anger with George walking out before he kills Vick.

George's labor and improvements on the farm over the last ten years have made Vick's land worth twice as much as it was when he began farming it, but Vick acknowledges no indebtedness to George. Vick's advice is to go on relief, but George will abandon the farm before doing that. Vick's only response is, "Put up or get out, that's all. I can't afford to carry you without getting a decent share of the crop money." The relationship between George and Vick is emblematic of the larger problem for farmers in the 1930s. The falling prices of land values and crops were increasing the number of tenant farmers with ever-greater obligations to the land owners, who dictated decisions about land use based on market analysis instead of farming acumen.

The Bones of Plenty contains many political references and views from a variety of characters, including an apparent Communist who shares a hospital room with Will Shepherd. Yet the book's only clear ideology is that the farmer is getting an unfair deal and needs to fight back against the rich men, the banks, the corporate interests, the railroads, the government, and anything else that is trying to run American agriculture. George's anger is too all-inclusive to allow him to focus on any coherent plan of action. He often speaks about making war on the "enemy" and occasionally addresses others about the need to work together to fight. At the end, however, he realizes that he has done nothing much and that the one occasion in which he threatened armed resistance ended in compromising his good name. By avoiding giving George an easy ideological position, Hudson is able to express the moral and economic wrongs at work in this system without reducing the difficulty of the struggle or prescribing overly simple explanations of its causes or cures. Even the banker who runs away with $2,000, a typical setup for a villain, was a victim of the debts farmers could not repay to him, not to mention the prejudice he experienced from the townspeople. Hudson maintains a vision of the daunting complexity of the interactions of drought, depression, international trade relations, small verses large banks, and the limits of a capitalist emphasis on competition and profit as a self-evident rationale for business practice.

Hudson's portrayal of the stress on family life in the homes of the Custers and the Shepherds is stripped of sentimentality. There are no Ma Joads in this novel and no optimism that the people will go on. George is legitimately angry at the unfairness of an economic system that takes his hard work and gives so little in return, yet his abusiveness of others makes him cruel. Hudson balances the reader's responses to the characters, especially to George, by telling much of the story through the eyes of his young daughter, Lucy. Lucy takes after her father, and they are close in many ways, but she is frequently a victim of his harshness and anger. Because she loves her father, Lucy tends to believe that the punishment she receives is somehow her fault. This narrative strategy allows us to see George's behavior from more than one set of eyes. More importantly, Lucy's turmoil and tears remind us of the emotionally damaging consequences to largely voiceless children wreaked by psychic violence in a desperate family.

George has none of the kindness and grace that Will Shepherd brought to his home. The son of an abusive father, whom he hated, George is harsh and demanding of his daughter Lucy. When Lucy fails to manage the challenging chores he requires of her, he whips her brutally with a razor strop. In one memorable episode, he puts her in charge of moving the cows to another field and driving them home at milking time. When Rachel protests that the job is too much for a seven-year-old child, George boasts that he herded cows when he was *five*! When Lucy starts herding the cows home, the family dog decides to run at them in play. The cows break into a run, knock down a fence, and get into a field of her father's wheat. George beats the dog and then moves on to his daughter, whipping her until she is screaming in pain.

The damage does not stop with Lucy. George's treatment of his daughter inspires Rachel to reflect on how "the man she had married became a beast" and to consider what she could do if she left him. George tries to justify himself by asserting, "I'm not going to raise a kid that doesn't obey me. Absolute obedience *must* be required of a child! Otherwise, they grow up spoiled rotten." As always, George needs to prove he was right and the actual victim in this episode: "If a man can't count on his own family for help . . . I don't see how he can be expected to make a go of it." He tells Rachel, "Your father spoiled *you*, and you want *me* to spoil *her*." Rachel retaliates, "I *love* my father! And just how did *you* feel about *yours*?"

Ten years of trying to deal with George's anger and self-justifications have eroded the love Rachel once felt for her husband. She refuses to argue with him, hoping that her silence will "make him feel that he ha[s] won." Her silence has the opposite effect on him, however, and he feels "defeated" by it: "It left him alone, with his anger gone, to hear again the things he had said, without so much as one culpable word of hers to recall and cling to in his search for justification. He had to bear the guilty aftermath of his rages all by himself." George reminds one of Frank Shabata in Cather's *O Pioneers!*, who felt Marie's happy nature was a betrayal of him. George, too, wants Rachel to take his side, to share his fury, to "say something that would commit herself to him." If she would admit that she was afraid, that she could not get along without him, if she would cry, he would know he had control of her. Rachel realizes that she no longer is committed to George in her heart, and her distance from her husband widens into a distaste for maleness in general.

The troubled family life of the Custers is initially in contrast to the good will and calm that prevails in the more financially secure home of Will and Rose Shepherd. Until Will is diagnosed with an incurable cancer, their biggest worry is their son, Stuart, an erratic young man with an alcohol problem and a compulsion to run from the constraints of life on the farm. He often feels closed in by his home and panics to get away. Feeling most "alone among people he kn[ows]," he only finds relief in liquor or hurrying somewhere else "so that he [will] only be alone among people he [*doesn't*] know." His parents are forgiving in nature and maintain hope that he will go to college and make something of himself. The reader is left guessing at the end of the novel whether Stuart will prove to be a weak reed in a strong wind or a surprisingly responsible and hardworking man who will successfully run his father's farm.

Stuart's marriage also leaves us wondering about the woman he brings home to his bitterly disappointed mother. He marries Annie Finley, who says she is pregnant with his child. The community views Annie's family as white trash, but in her cooler moments, Stuart's rather-evangelical mother, Rose, can feel pity for the family because "the Finleys belonged to a class of people that could not be said to have had any real chance in the world." Rose considers Annie a trollop and, in an angry outburst, calls her a "slut" with the "mark of the Beast" (Satan) on her. The freckled Annie looks "exactly like a saloon waitress," which was her job, but Hudson's portrayal of her stresses that she keeps herself exceptionally clean, works hard, and gives all her earnings to her family. Rose feels degraded, however, to be *related* to her, and Annie represents for her the "filth" of the world that surrounds her and is now living in her home. Whether Annie is a slut or just another good-hearted "hired girl" or even a Rose of Sharon who will give the milk of kindness to the starving poor is left for the reader to imagine.

Left with nothing but the bones of plenty, the Custer family prepares to move west. The farm is gone, the sale of their possessions is a disappointment, and the car and trailer are packed to leave behind everything they have ever known. George admits to himself that he never even found, let alone fought, the enemy, that he "hadn't so much as reconnoitered the battlefield before he was down." The move almost shatters Rachel's sanity. She cannot imagine who they are if they leave behind all the roots that gave them identity. They are people without a mailing address, just another "shiftless roving family" like the Finleys in the eyes of the world. The reader may well remember that this setting is only 1934 and that the Great Depression would drag on for more than six years before World War II would bring a revitalizing war economy. Sometimes characters in a book can be so real that we worry about them beyond the last page of the text. George, Rachel, and Lucy are fictionalized, but there were real people behind them through the autobiographical parallels with the author's life, and there were many more real people like them of whom we cannot sketch a biography. Readers who wonder what happens to the Custers after they leave North Dakota may want to explore Hudson's collection of short stories for more fictionalized insights and experiences drawn from her personal experience of the Great Depression.

The war on the enemy never gets organized in *The Bones of Plenty*. Mari Sandoz's *Capital City* focuses on the forces that hold the power and those who organize against them. She takes up the struggle of desperate farmers and striking truckers in conflict with the bankers, politicians, and upper class of owners. Her enemies control the money, the government, and the law,

Fig. 12. Mari Sandoz in her apartment. RG 1274 PH 0-12. Courtesy of the Nebraska State Historical Society.

and they have no hesitation about using their power to protect their interests from the poor people who are threatening their order by demanding better pay for their work.

Sandoz (1896–1966) was from the Sand Hills of Nebraska. She is best known for *Old Jules*, a portrait of her pioneering but abusive father and for her numerous books about Native Americans, such as *Crazy Horse* and *Cheyenne Autumn*, which also became a popular film. In *Capital City* Sandoz is concerned about the rising violent clashes of rich and poor that bore many of the earmarks of Fascism. *Capital City* was published in 1939, the same year as *The Grapes of Wrath* and also the year that Germany invaded Poland to officially begin World War II. She based her story of protest in part on the march on the capitol building in Lincoln, Nebraska, in 1933. In the novel the locale is

"Franklin, Kanewa," a city in a generic plains state whose name is a composite of syllables from Kansas, Nebraska, and Iowa. Anyone even vaguely familiar with Lincoln will recognize Franklin's similarity to that particular capital city. Certainly the people of Lincoln did when the book was published, and Sandoz was given a very hard time by the locals.

Capital City is a scathing book with very few gray areas between right and wrong, but it is instructive of the anger in the Great Depression that drove people into the extreme polarizations of class, status, and politics. Behind the anger of those in need was terrible fear, the fear of losing everything one had worked for, the fear of being homeless and hungry, the fear even of surviving. Despite the frequency of "remembered" tales about feeding tramps on the back porch, those who were comfortable were often angered by the demands of those in need. As Studs Terkel's oral history of the Great Depression, *Hard Times* (1970), shows us, people who have known such fears never forget them and wear the scars for the rest of their lives.

The people in *Hard Times* are remembering events from thirty and forty years ago, but Sandoz's novel was written in medias res. Not only was the desperation of the Great Depression not yet the past, but the world of the late 1930s was, to paraphrase W. B. Yeats, "slouching" toward "the second coming" of a world war. *Capital City* is full of Sandoz's anxieties about the rise of Nazism in Germany and the repressive climate in the United States that looks to her too much like what she is seeing in Europe. In Franklin, Kanewa, the leftists are the good people (the poor, the strikers, the farmers, the journalists), and the right wingers are the bad people (the bankers, the railroad executives, the elected politicians, the "Gold Shirts," and the Ku Klux Klan). The strong-arm tactics of the powerful against the resisters in Franklin act out on a small scale the repressive force that Germany was using to reshape itself and later all of Europe. Sandoz's prescient understanding of the nature of the threat in the Fascist movements in Europe and her correlations in the United States are reasons this novel continues to have relevance.

Though the capital city of Franklin is the main character in Sandoz's novel, she populates it with a wide variety of characters who embody the class strata within the town. At the bottom of the ladder are the squatters who live in shacks and shelter houses on the edge of the city, or even in caves, like "Coot," the bankrupted old curmudgeon who once owned the leading bank. The people of the Polish Bottoms are poor but have some means of sustaining themselves as a community. Around the university are intellectuals and professionals, including Abigail Allerton, the Sandoz-like novelist whose book about Franklin excites and angers the town. A mix of striking truckers and farmers are treated mainly as groups who parade in protest. The imported strikebreakers and gunmen for the companies add violence to the mix. A group of mean-spirited young men, mainly from the best families, are members of the Fascist Gold Shirts. The class structure is topped by the "best families," who helped found the town but have lived with riches and privilege long enough to be corrupted by them. Circulating in and among all of them are the politicians who are candidates for governor or senator.

Sandoz's chief character is Hamm Rufe, an assumed name of a writer who is actually the son of the Hammond family, one of the wealthiest and most notable families in Franklin. Hamm has fallen out with his family, however, and is on the side of the people who are protesting. By connecting Hamm with the social and financial leaders of the town, Sandoz is able to present this story through multiple class and political perspectives. The Hammonds and the Welles are the old families who built the town and still set the social bar for others.

Among the social climbers are the nouveau riche Tyndales, whose daughter, Mollie, threatens to undermine the family's social ambitions by falling in love with Burt, the son of "the trashy Parrs," who is allied with the leftists.

The political structure includes three candidates for governor. They are the socially respectable conservative Republican, incumbent governor Johnson Ryon; the liberal Carl Halzer, known as the Bull of Bashan and hero of the strikers and farmers; and the demagogic Dr. D. C. "Charley" Stetbettor, the far right candidate allied with the Fascist Gold Shirts and the cross-burning Ku Klux Klan. His motto is "America for Americans, no Indians included." The Gold Shirts, Franklin's version of the Brown Shirts of Hitler's Germany, the Black Shirts of Mussolini's Italy, and the Blue Shirts of Ireland, echo the Fascist talk of Hitler, including the virulent anti-Semitism and hatred of foreigners.

At times, it may seem that Sandoz is playing with a heavy hand in some of her characterizations of the right, but the rhetoric about "Reds" and "Jews" was common across the plains and has periodically appeared in U.S. politics in figures such as Huey Long, Father Coughlin, George Wallace, Joe McCarthy, and others even more contemporary. The fact that Sandoz was also watching the rise of Hitler's Germany during the time she was writing *Capital City* adds some moral weight to the ugly drama of Kanewa, which echoes some of the same ideas and language flourishing in Germany.

Sandoz uses a short subplot to illustrate how Fascist ideas can infect a community. Two young refugee boys come to Franklin. The father of nine-year-old José was killed in the civil war in Spain, and Isaac is a Jew who escaped from Germany. At school, twelve-year-old Isaac is taunted with "Ikey, kikey / Kill a Christy— / Drink a baby's blood," and José's father is presumed to be a "Red." Letter writers to the local newspaper complain that such refugees are "flooding the country with undesirable aliens and taking the bread out of the mouths of white men." The do-gooders are "bringing in Reds and Jews to cut the throats of our sons and rape our daughters!" The boys, who are friends, are deliberately struck and killed by a hit-and-run driver of a red convertible. There is only one red convertible licensed in Franklin, and it belongs to the son of the man who owns Franklin Mills. The son, also said to belong to the Gold Shirts, immediately leaves for California in the car, and while everyone in town knows who owns the car, nothing is done beyond the gossip.

Sandoz gives us more than enough characters to fill this town of sixty thousand, but the town itself is in the starring role. Early in the novel, she characterizes Franklin as a prostitute and as a parasitic capital city that produces nothing, lives off the state government and the university, and has "a hand in every Goddam pocket in the state." Within Sandoz's novel, Abigail Allerton, who writes a novel exposing the corruption in the capital city of Franklin, finds that the wealth of the city was derived from the free land made available by the federal government. The land, especially after the Homestead Act in 1862, was "the country's hundred fifty year long WPA project for the unemployed," Abigail says. She describes how when hard times came in the 1890s, "you could buy up the country if you had fifty cents ahead," and argues, "That's how the Franklin National got going—and the rest of the town." The banks took the wealth from the soil, too, leaving it "all skinned down like a bald man's head, and holding no more water—."

Although the leading families of Franklin like to think that the role of their town is "to envision and disseminate the highest attributes of cultural living" to the state, Sandoz portrays it as "a community that had nothing at all for the young but to think the thoughts of the old." The idealistic students who come to the university soon leave, and the first generation that came to America for freedom and to build a good life is dead. Both Hamm and Abigail lament what the town has become: "The Midwestern capital cities were not only parasites, but poisonous parasites, insinuating their paralysis into the bodies of their states." The Ku Klux Klan is burning crosses at the homes of Jews, and the climate is so toxic that even the League of Women Voters is under attack.

The violent clashes between the haves and the have-nots reach a climax when the Gold Shirts set fire to some of the shacks in the Polish section, and the fire spreads rapidly to several homes, killing one invalid man. Soon after the fire, the tension between strikers and companies breaks out in armed conflict, and when the demagogue Stetbettor wins the governor's office, all hopes for settling anything with negotiations collapse. Things are so dangerous that Mollie Tyndale's father tells her and Burt to get out of Franklin for their safety, and Hamm's mother, Hallie, disturbed by the fires, tries to exercise her influence to halt the charge of the Gold Shirts and hired finks from attacking the strikers. The Gold Shirts call her "an old She-Red" and strike her with a gun. Hamm jerks her out of the way of a second blow, which he takes in the face instead. This murderously violent scene is, fittingly, interrupted by the onslaught of a crowd of raucous football fans celebrating the university's triumphant homecoming victory.

Sandoz's attack on the culture of Franklin is always biting, but occasionally she manages some amusing satire. The novel begins with the unexpected death of Cobbie Welles, a leading socialite. Cobbie is found dead in the men's restroom, dressed in satin knee britches, "feet sticking out from under the door of the can." He is wearing satin knee britches because he was to be part of the annual coronation of a new emperor and empress of Kanewa in which a successful older businessman is crowned emperor, dons an ermine robe, and escorts the new empress, a pretty young girl dressed in virginal white, to their thrones. Sandoz based the farcical coronation court on a quasi-Arthurian pageant held each year by Omaha society. In the Omaha gala, the Knights of Aksarben are part of a mythical realm of knights and ladies wearing eighteenth-century knee pants and ball gowns. In Sandoz's version, the "satin britches" worn by men of the coronation court are pulled "over potbellies or legs too bowed to keep a pig in an alley." ("Aksarben" is "Nebraska" spelled backward. Some folks in South Sioux City apparently thought this was so clever that they created "Atokad Downs," a horse-racing track that closed in 2012.

Capital City is an ambitious book that is flawed with too many characters, few of which are drawn with much psychological depth. Unlike Hudson's rich portraits, which capture the reader, Sandoz's characters from all walks of life rarely engage us. Still, the story itself has the power of historical drama revealed in all its ugliness and pain. Sandoz researched the novel by reading newspapers from various states. The events in Franklin are generic to many of the plains states during the 1930s. The kinds of demagoguery, anti-Semitism, red-baiting, and violence against those who defy the establishment in this book of the 1930s are present in other novels and stories about the Depression years on the Great Plains. Fear and anger existed on both sides of the economic divide, and where people feel threatened, they often resort to force. As all three of these novels show us, the power of the haves against the have-nots is never an even match.

Sandoz's *Capital City* might be less believable today if the violence that accompanied the conflicts of the 1930s had not been repeated in the 1950s with McCarthyism or in the 1960s and 1970s with civil rights and the war in Vietnam. How different is the society that will wink at running down children from Spain and Germany from the one that bombs Sunday school children in Birmingham, Alabama; shoots students at Kent State; or guns down a study group in a Charleston, South Carolina, church? I raise this question to suggest that books like *Capital City* have an importance to our understanding of history, despite the fact that they can be uncomfortable to read and often possess an emphatic moral tone that may annoy. Sandoz asks us to question if "we" are not also "they," if the ordinariness of daily life in our towns may not also mask a dark anger that can break out in meanness and violation of others, if within power lies the easy temptation of abuse. *Capital City* belongs to that genre of novels like Sinclair Lewis's *Main Street* or *Babbitt* and Upton Sinclair's *The Jungle*. Such novels possess a memorable power through what they expose, and this power trumps the deficiencies of form or style.

Stories of the Great Depression on the plains are so vividly pictured in literature, film, and photography that it can be easy to forget that the Depression was nationwide, even worldwide, and that people lost homes and jobs all across the country. An equally iconic American image of the Great Depression was that of people committing suicide by jumping from the tall buildings of New York. Yet there was a singularity in the experience of the Great Plains that separates it from the rest of the nation. Its economy was almost wholly reliant on agriculture, and the financial crisis overlapped with a disastrous drought that dried up the life in the land. The visible conditions of drought and dust were an externalization in the landscape of the devastated economy. A shady street of houses in Pennsylvania or Mississippi might look much the same in 1934 as it did in 1924 and as it would in 1944, whatever the desperation and ruin of the residents within. But the drought-stricken small towns, farms, and highways of Oklahoma, Kansas, Nebraska, the Dakotas, and Saskatchewan did not. Losing one's money was terrifying, but the darkness of a dust storm was an added horror, as was the sense of violation as the dirt sifted into every corner of one's home. To live with drought is to live with death. Drought is supposed to be a temporary thing; when it goes on from year to year, the laws of nature seem upended. These novels bring home to us something of the experience the people of the plains must have felt when the very forces of life in the natural world betrayed the bountiful gifts of the earth.

CHAPTER SIX

City Living on the Edge

Day upon day and year upon year, O city, walking your streets,
Where you hold me enchain'd a certain time, refusing to give me up;
. . . .
(O I see what I sought to escape, confronting, reversing my cries;
I see my own soul trampling down what it ask'd for.)
—Walt Whitman, "Give Me the Splendid Silent Sun"

Despite the familiar images of empty spaces and big skies that stretch the width of the horizon, the Great Plains had several developing cities in the nineteenth century. Today, in many areas, cities account for the majority of the inhabitants, and the population increasingly shifts from rural areas into these cities. Several plains cities have metropolitan areas of more than a million inhabitants. Historically these cities developed along rivers or rail lines and became centers of commerce, transportation, energy, and meatpacking. Today they are all transportation hubs for a radius that may sprawl two hundred or more miles beyond the metropolitan area. To envision the plains without its cities is to be blind to an important part of the history and culture of the region.

Plains cities mainly dot the borders of the region along rivers and early railroad centers. Tulsa, metropolitan Kansas City, Omaha, Sioux Falls, Fargo, Winnipeg, Calgary, Denver, Amarillo, and Lubbock encircle the massive amount of farm and ranch land of the area. Though Fargo and Sioux Falls have populations well below two hundred thousand, they are still the largest cities in North Dakota and South Dakota. Only the cities of Wichita, Lincoln, Bismarck, and Oklahoma City are located deeper into the plains, and of those, only Oklahoma City and Wichita are the largest cities in their state. Not technically located on the Great Plains, the Twin Cities of Minneapolis and St. Paul, with a population of about 3.5 million, constitute the largest metropolitan area between Chicago and Los Angeles. Minneapolis is a magnet for commercial interests in the northern Great Plains and for migration to the city both for the young looking for opportunity and for those who have given up on farm life.

Most of these cities are also the sites on the plains where Jewish, African American, and Latino populations cluster. According to the most recent census, more than 70 percent of Native Americans are likely to be urban residents today. Denver has one of the largest Latino concentrations in the United States at almost 32 percent. Although the plains have always been home to many white European ethnic groups, minority populations greatly enhance the diversity of its cities.

The cities have most often hovered on the edges of plains literature. Marie Shabata in *O Pioneers!* is from Omaha, and Frank courts her there. The characters in Kent Haruf's fictional town of Holt, Colorado, go in and out of Denver with the various changes of their lives. Katherine Anne Porter's famed "Pale Horse, Pale Rider" is set in Denver during the 1918 influenza epidemic. In Cather's *The Song of the Lark* Thea Kronborg visits Denver, and Doctor Archie moves there. Several distinguished writers have, however, given us stories that rely on a city environment. Tillie Olsen's *Yonnondio* (1974), Meridel Le Sueur's *The Girl* (1978), and Rilla Askew's *Fire in Beulah* (2001) are set, respectively, in Omaha, Minneapolis–St. Paul,

Fig. 13. Tillie Olsen with Linda Pratt at the 1994 Nebraska Literature
Festival in Omaha. Courtesy of the photographer, David McCleery.

and Tulsa, in the 1920s and 1930s. These novels have political or historical implications and focus on the plight of the poor and oppressed. The main characters are all women or young girls caught up in the turmoil of events around them over which they have little or no control. They begin life in a rural setting and migrate to the city to escape the poverty of the farm, only to encounter mean streets and discrimination. Their stories have little resemblance to any conventional romance of the country girl who goes to the city to find her fortune.

Tillie Olsen (1912–2007) was born Tybile Lerner in Omaha, Nebraska, in a family of Russian Jewish immigrants. Her parents, Sam and Ida Lerner, fled the Minsk area of Russia in 1905 to escape possible reprisals as suspected revolutionaries. The Jewish population in Omaha was estimated to be ten thousand in 1917, a sizable number for any plains city. Temple Israel was founded in 1871, and the *Jewish Press* in 1920. Olsen's parents were active Socialist Party members, and she grew up in a home filled with politics. The Lerners were not, in Olsen's words, "Temple Jews," and she attended the Socialist Sunday School instead. Tillie dropped out of Central High in Omaha in 1929 to join the Communist movement, a source of grief to her Socialist parents. She lived most of her adult life in California, where she married fellow comrade Jack Olsen (originally named Olshansky) in 1944. In 1961 she published a novella, *Tell Me a Riddle*, and in 1974 she reworked material from drafts created in 1934 for *Yonnondio*. Both books are fiction but draw heavily from the life of her own family, who lived in Omaha for about forty years.

Tell Me a Riddle concerns an elderly Jewish couple who emigrated from Russia in 1905. The story is set in the 1950s as the wife approaches death. She reflects on how the exigencies of work and rearing seven children displaced pursuing the ideals of their youth. Both Rölvaag and Cather gave voice in some characters to the longing for the Old World and its ways, but the sense of loss in *Tell Me a Riddle* is more than just a longing for home and customs. It explores the cost of compromising beliefs and distorting traditions to accommodate the demands of assimilation in American culture. Many immigrants came to the United States in order to escape oppression, not for love of America or even materialistic goals of getting ahead. During World Wars I and II many personal histories of political struggle were suppressed, even within the family, as people sought to avoid ethnic, political, or financial discrimination. During the Cold War years, any suspicion that one harbored any "un-American" beliefs or was a "radical" in the past could lead to harassment and even prison. *Tell Me a Riddle* reminds us that the price of assimilation was for many a profound and painful loss of one's core identity and that the loss extended into the second and third generations.

In *Yonnondio*, subtitled "From the Thirties," the Holbrook family moves to a city like Omaha after failing at farming in South Dakota. Olsen drew on her family's experience with farming near Mead, Nebraska, where they located after the 1913 Omaha tornado devastated their neighborhood. She was also familiar with meatpacking in Omaha and in Kansas City, where Olsen did political work for a few months. The title *Yonnondio* is from Walt Whitman's poem of the same name. Whitman interpreted the Iroquois word to mean a lament or dirge, and Olsen uses it in that sense to write the story of the people of whom there was "no picture, poem, [or] statement, passing them to the future." Whitman's poem is about the American Indian, but Olsen's is about the nameless, poor working families whose lives go unheralded and unrecorded.

The Depression-era story of the Holbrook family begins in a mining town in Wyoming, but soon the family moves to a farm in Zell, South Dakota. The prairie that stretches before them seems to promise "joy and freedom illimitable," "a new life" with "two twin stars" hanging in the sky overhead. Like Sam Lerner in Mead, Jim Holbrook is a tenant farmer, and his neighbor is quick to tell him, "Tenant farmin is the only thing worse than farmin your own . . . tenant farmin, bad or good year, the bank swallows everything up and keeps you owin 'em." Farming does not turn out well for the Holbrooks, and like many others who failed on the prairie, they continue their reverse migration eastward to Omaha.

Olsen draws on memories of her own young life in the portrait of Mazie, the stargazing child awakening to the wonders and terrors of her world. For Mazie the time on the farm is transforming. The beauty and lessons of nature are enhanced and translated for her by her conversations with Elias Caldwell, an elderly farmer. On his deathbed he advises her to "live," not merely "exist," to know what's real, and to "remember" that "everything, the nourishment, the roots you need, are where you are now." Caldwell gives the child his books, but Mazie's father sells them before she can get them. Still, the hunger to read and know is deeply planted in the girl. As despair takes over the house, the once seductive green of the landscape becomes "ugly," "patches of soiled snow oozing away, leaving the ground like great dirty sores between; scabs of old leaves that like a bruise hid[ing] the violets underneath." Trees are "fat with oily buds, and the swollen breasts of prairie."

Life in the city will make it very difficult for a stargazing child to see the beauty of nature. To her the city is loud with the "rasps and shrieks" of "monster trucks" and streetcars that shake the houses as they pass. Even more disturbing are the "human noises—weeping and scolding and tired words that slip out in monosyllables" that "can scarcely be called human." Worst of all, "the fog of stink smothers down over it all—so solid, so impenetrable, no other smell lives in it." The terrible smell is from the stockyards, and "that stench is a reminder—a proclamation—*I rule here*. It speaks for the packinghouses, heart of all that moves in these streets."

Olsen's meatpacking city is home to a polyglossic population of workers from economically depressed areas including Ireland, Italy, Eastern Europe, Russia, and the American South. When Mazie and her brother go to the new school, they are overwhelmed at the lesson in "Na-tion-al-it-ies" and the many black and honey-colored faces. Unlike the predominantly rural population of Catholic or Protestant whites who came to the plains from Germany, Scandinavia, and other parts of the United States, places like Omaha and Kansas City attracted many African Americans in the Great Migration. In a state that has a 4 percent African American population, Omaha today has a black population of nearly 14 percent; Kansas City is closer to 30 percent. Chicago, Omaha, and Kansas City were for decades the three largest meatpacking cities in the United States, and by 1955 Omaha was the number one meatpacking city in the United States before it, too, phased out its stockyards in 2000.

The stench of the stockyards in the novel is a palpable embodiment of life's ugly realities that now surround Mazie. The smell arising from the stock pens and rendering operations reaches inescapably into home and school and the streets. Some characters describe it as smelling like vomit, and when the summer sun beats down, the oppressive heat and odor together can literally sicken people. Her father, Jim, is not lucky enough (!) to get a job in the packinghouse and must work in the sewers, where he spends the day underground in wet and smell. At home with four children, Anna is ill with pregnancy and miscarriage, washing diapers and trying to cook meals in a hot kitchen where no air stirs.

Mazie tries hard to shut out her new environment by daydreaming about the farm and its imagined serenity. Walking in a daydream, she bumps into a stranger who angrily shoves her to the pavement, spits on her, and calls her a "stinking little bitch." In her terror the streets become a nightmare of people with faces distorted by laughing at her. She runs to the top of the street, looks down, and sees where, "like a hog," "a great hulk of building wallowed." Mazie studies the sign she sees: "A-R-M-O-U-R-S [the] gray letters shrieked. Armours, said Mazie over and over: Armoursarmoursarmours." In this dramatic moment of recognition, the child confronts her reality and the corporate giant that *rules*. The stench of the packing plant is also the sign of its exploitation of the people who work in it.

Olsen's description of work in the packinghouse sounds like some factory line we might find in an updated image from Dante's *Inferno*:

> Hell. Figures half-seen through hissing vapor, live steam cloud from great scalding vats. Hogs dangling, dancing along the convey, 300, 350 an hour . . . to the shuddering drum of the skull crush machine, in the spectral vapor clouds. . . . Year-round breathing with open mouth, learning to pant shallow to endure the excrement reek of offal, the smothering stench from the blood house below. Windowless: bleared dank light. . . . Heat of hell year round, for low on their heads from the lowering ceiling, the plant's steam machinery. Incessant slobber down of its oil and scalding water onto their rubber caps, into their rubber galoshes.

The endless routines and working conditions in the packinghouses are so horrific and deadening that the workers begin to feel that they, too, are "steamed boiled broiled fried cooked. Geared, meshed." Yet the description of Anna, sick at home, surrounded by four children and the smell of wet diapers, trying to cook in temperatures of 110 degrees and not breathe in the smell, is almost equally hellish.

Gradually Mazie becomes a city girl, running about on the streets with her friend Jinella, who makes a pretend palace from a tent and jewelry from cans and other shiny things found on the dump. The girls pretend to be vamps they have seen in the movies and magazines. Too young they learn about their bodies from street chants like

> Girl go to London, go to France
> Evrybody sees your pants
> Girl shimmy, shimmy shimmyhigh
> Evrybody sees your pie

While Mazie scavenges the city dump for treasures and chases an ice truck for falling slivers, her mother still holds on to her futile dreams of giving her a good education and feeding the mind of the bright and lovely child with books and music.

Yonnondio ends without conclusion but not without an image of a moment's grace. With temperatures reaching 107 degrees, Anna has spent the afternoon canning peaches and making jelly, juggling baby Bess on one hip, and stirring the boiling pot on the stove. Her children have been whining and squabbling but eventually fall asleep. Jim comes in from work, exhausted beyond speaking, and wets himself down. But Mazie awakes to see rainbows on the wall from sunlight through a prism casting radiance on her mother's hair. Baby Bess discovers her competence to bang a jar lid against a table. Will comes in with a borrowed radio for all to hear. The air changes, bringing temperatures tomorrow that will be tolerable. As unbearable as the heat, the smell, the poverty, the unwanted pregnancies, and the horrible work are, the Holbrooks are surviving, and isolate moments of love and beauty still visit their lives.

Mazie has the protection of her parents, frail as it is, but what of the young single women who go alone to the cities in search of opportunity? Meridel Le Sueur's *The Girl* was drafted

Fig. 14. Meridel Le Sueur as a young woman reading under a tree. Courtesy of the Minnesota Historical Society.

in 1939 but revised in 1977 and published as a novel in 1978. It is set in 1936–37 in Minneapolis–St. Paul, where Le Sueur made her home. Le Sueur (1900–1996) was born in Iowa, but her childhood was spent in Perry, Oklahoma, and Fort Scott, Kansas, where her mother, Marian Wharton, was a teacher in the People's College, a left-wing school for the masses.

In 1917 Marian married Arthur Le Sueur. He had been elected mayor of Minot, North Dakota, in 1911, on the Socialist ticket. Like Tillie Olsen, Meridel Le Sueur joined the Communists. She had many stories in leading magazines and the Communist press. Party officials were critical of her interest in women's lives and considered her fiction too lyrical. During the Cold War years, she supported herself by writing commercially successful children's books published by Knopf. In the 1970s and 1980s a new generation of feminist readers rediscovered Le Sueur, and *The Girl* and *I Hear Men Talking* were published.

In a journalistic piece in *New Masses* (1932), "Women on the Breadlines," Le Sueur notes:

> It's one of the great mysteries of the city where women go when they are out of work and hungry. There are not many women in the breadline. There are no flophouses for women as there are for men, where a bed can be had for a quarter or less. You don't see women lying around on the floor at the mission in the free flops. . . . What happens to them? Where do they go?

The Girl, first drafted in 1939, gives us some answers to that question. The novel is written as the first-person narrative of the titular Girl, whose name is never mentioned. She comes to the city from the country to relieve her desperately poor family of one mouth to feed. When she gets a waitress job in a bar, she steps into a demimonde of city corruption, crime, and sexual pressure with no experience to guide her.

The Girl might be called feminist crime fiction, but the bank robbers, bootleggers, and prostitutes in it rarely fit any of the conventions of the genre. Clara, a prostitute, is a delicately beautiful and fragile young woman with a generous heart and a body wracked by thirteen abortions. Belle, who helps run the bar with her husband, the bootlegger, is a kind but strong woman who dearly loves her rough husband. Butch is the handsome young man who pressures the Girl sexually, strikes her on occasion, and robs a bank. Yet he dreams of getting enough money to lease a gas station and marry her. Working at the bar, the Girl gets to know these people. The only hardened criminal is Ganz, the big boss who exploits this group of struggling people who work just outside the law, trying to survive. In the one major crime the men undertake, they prove to be grossly inept and wind up shooting each other and leaving behind all the money they had just stolen from the bank.

The novel belongs to the women, however, and Le Sueur gives us an insightful portrait of their supportive lives together and the pleasures and terrors of their sexual relations with men. Until the 1960s, women writers rarely wrote candidly about sexuality, and Le Sueur's account of the Girl's sexual coming of age would have been startling, perhaps scandalous, to a 1930s audience. By the time it was finally published in 1978, it was welcomed by a new audience. As a young writer, Le Sueur had read the novels of D. H. Lawrence. Lawrence tried "to break the idea of sex as commodity," she told me, by suffusing sexuality with mysticism. While she felt liberated by his candid descriptions of sexual relationships in literature, she thought he did not fully understand the woman's experience. Le Sueur's men have no mysticism about sexuality and are often brutish with women. The Girl is surprised that her first sexual experience hurts and wonders, "Had I failed?"

The Girl learns from her mother and Belle that there can be great joy in sex when one loves her partner and from Clara that one can enjoy sex without love if the woman's sexual responses are considered. In a delicate conversation with her mother, the Girl tries to find out what her mother means when she says of her husband, "He was good to me." The Girl's experience of her father was of a man who "only had to look at me to want to hit me good and plenty." Her mother describes a man of tender affection who was proud of her as a wife and mother. Poor as she was and as embittered as her husband became, her mother hopes that the Girl will "marry a man like [her] papa and have children." She tells her daughter, "It's a fierce feeling you have for your husband and children like you could feed them your body, and chop yourself up into little pieces.... To know each other, touch, sing, feel it in your breast and throat. You have to live it and die it and then you know it."

After the fatal robbery, the women are left alone. Clara is dying, her health ruined by abortions; Belle is bootlegging a little and trying to get on a relief program; and the Girl, pregnant with no money and no husband, is applying to get milk and oranges to protect the development of her unborn child. They become the city's homeless people. The Girl tells us:

The streets used to be only something you walked through to get someplace else, but now they are home to me, and I walk around, and walk in stores and look at all the people, or I sit in the relief station waiting to see the case worker, and I sit there close to other women and men, and I look, I feed off their faces. They feed me, I don't feel scared when I am sitting there and it is warm and I am close to the bodies of others. I don't know them but I know them all.

Fig. 15. Rilla Askew. Photograph by Ted Waddell. Courtesy of Rilla Askew.

The official society regards these women as undesirables, and the relief agency recommends that the Girl be sterilized and that Clara be given shock treatments. With the help of other women, the Girl escapes the people who should be helping her. The women band together in an abandoned warehouse to survive the winter.

The Girl's sense of kinship with the other homeless people leads her into the circle of the Workers Alliance, a left-wing organization of people on relief. The Workers Alliance embodies the collective oneness she has learned living on the streets. Her friendship with Belle and Clara has taught her the strength of solidarity with other women. The Workers Alliance and the character of Amelia, one of the Alliance's officers, are perhaps strained notes in the novel to satisfy Le Sueur's sense that her fiction should address the agenda of the Communist Party. If the ending is a little too ideologically neat, the arc of the story traces how the Girl opens herself to living and touching others, to seeing goodness and strength in women whom society may dismiss as worthless. Le Sueur has given us a story of lives lived in the shadows and known to most readers only as statistics. Homeless women have more shelters today than they had in 1937, but stories like the Girl's are still a reality every day in our cities.

Olsen and Le Sueur write the stories of lives that are largely unknown. Rilla Askew (b. 1951) writes a story that many knew but wanted to forget. Her award-winning 2001 novel, *Fire in Beulah*, is about the 1921 race riot in Tulsa, Oklahoma, that the city tried to expunge from its history. Askew is a native of Oklahoma and now teaches at the University of Oklahoma. She received her master of fine arts degree from Brooklyn College and has published four widely reviewed and award-winning novels.

In 1989 Askew came across a reference to the 1921 riot in a biography of Richard Wright, noted author of *Native Son* and *Black Boy*. She was startled that she had never heard of the 1921 riot, though she grew up in nearby Bartlesville. When she tried to research it, she found that the copies of the *Tulsa World* and *Tulsa Tribune* from May through September of 1921 were missing from the archives. The story was front-page news in newspapers across the country, however, and she also found extensive coverage of it in the black newspapers archived at the Ralph Ellison Library in Oklahoma City.

The Tulsa race riot of 1921 is the single worst race riot in American history. Askew has said that what began as a race riot ended as a pogrom. Scott Ellsworth's *Death in a Promised Land: The Tulsa Race Riot of 1921* (1982) meticulously reconstructs the events as the riot unfolded. The Greenwood District of Tulsa, with a population of roughly ten thousand, was one of the wealthiest black communities in the United

Fig. 16. Burning Will Brown's body after lynching in Omaha on September 28, 1919. RG 2281 PH 0-69. Courtesy of the Nebraska State Historical Society.

States. Some had dubbed it the Black Wall Street of America. After the end of World War I, however, a national climate of racial conflict had so intensified that the summer of 1919 was called the Red Summer because of all the blood that had been shed. While lynching was most common in the southern states where slavery had existed, lynching also happened in plains states. One Red Summer incident in Omaha resulted in the lynching of a young black man whose body was burned by the mob and the near-fatal lynching of the white mayor who tried to protect him but was luckily cut down before he died.

Oklahoma was home to numerous African Americans who had immigrated there after the end of slavery or who had once been slaves held by Native Americans from the Five Civilized Tribes when Oklahoma was Indian Territory. Oklahoma had a long history of lynching and burning and a Ku Klux Klan so powerful it could openly build its own three-story Beno Hall in 1922 in Tulsa. In 1911 an African American mother and son, Laura and L. D. Nelson, were hanged together from a bridge near Okemah. Another black man was hanged in 1920 in Oklahoma City. Tulsa's capacity for anger to turn to violence had already surfaced in the lynching in 1920 of Roy Belton, a white youth, and in another incident in which a mob had tarred and feathered seventeen local union leaders of the Industrial Workers of the World. Askew incorporates into the novel historical details of the Candler lynching in Oklahoma City and the Belton lynching in Tulsa to portray the climate of violence that motivated Greenwood's African American citizens to act to stop a lynching, despite a terrible fear of what kind of punishment whites might rain down on them.

As is often the case, the Greenwood riot grew out of a disputed minor incident when a black shoe shiner, Dick Rowland, tripped or stepped on a young white female elevator operator's foot as he exited. She screamed; he was arrested after being seen exiting the building. The headlines played up the incident, "Nab Negro for Attacking Girl," and rumors of rape and lynching began to circulate. Newspapers and others sent out a call for whites to come armed to fight against the armed blacks who had volunteered to help the sheriff protect the security of the jail. The ensuing violence destroyed Greenwood's black-owned businesses, burned some thirty-five city blocks, killed an estimated three hundred people, and led to the arrest of an additional six thousand black residents. Machine guns were fired, and even airplanes were employed to drop dynamite on Greenwood. The district was burned to the ground, and other blacks fled or were driven out of town. Ultimately, the young woman refused to press charges, and Rowland was freed, but not before the damage of the riot was done. No one was ever arrested from the thousands of whites who burned and killed over a sixteen-hour period. Not until 1996 was an official report commissioned by the Oklahoma legislature.

Askew's powerful novel portrays the anatomy of racism that fuels such destructive fires and then tries to blot them from memory. In the book, Roscoe Dunjee, the real-life black editor of Greenwood's *Black Dispatch*, says that such unspeakable events are "too horrible for us to remember. Too horrifying to forget." Askew structures the story around the relationship between two women—the well-off, white Althea Whiteside Dedmeyer, whose husband is a moderately successful oilman, and Graceful Whiteside, Althea's black domestic servant. For much of the novel, Graceful's life is so beyond Althea's interest or imagination that she does not realize they share a surname. Askew gives us "the single narrative of their bound-together lives" as the kinship and shared name become a metaphor for the racial world to which they are bound.

Althea is from a dirt-poor family in the country near Bristow, but she lies about her past so that no one, not even her husband, will know the truth. The book opens in 1900 with the gruesome birth of her brother, Japheth, when she is just twelve. The girl witnesses the horror at her mother's labor and hears her overwrought mother say to take "it" out and smash its head in. The girl tries to do so, and only the quick intervention of the black woman who had assisted in the birth saves the baby. "Aletha Jean," as she is known to her family, hates the poverty and fear of her childhood. Even though her family is not remarkably different from many other poor white families of the time, she is full of self-pity for "her imagined loss and grief, for having wanted, wanted all her life, and never got." Althea's most important lies are the ones she tells herself. She has learned to push "all uncomfortable recollections . . . to a confined corner of her mind" where she can dismiss them.

In the Dedmeyer home Graceful's face is studiously without animation, and she works at a steady but unhurried pace. The demanding Althea is angered by Graceful's lack of the desired emotional responses. Althea sees in her face "the sullen, resentful look of Negro pride," and at times, "she hate[s] the girl with a dead white heat." This is no Miss Scarlett and Mammy story, or even Skeeter and "the help." Althea believes that Graceful is her "silent, secret judge," and she is obsessed with her. Despite Althea's rage at the impenetrable Graceful, and Graceful's dislike of her officious and simpering employer, the life of each woman will change the other as they are both caught up in the racial turmoil of rape, lynching, and race war.

Askew's vision of racial oppression links it to one of its core causes—human greed. Slavery flourished because it provided the unpaid labor needed to enrich the American economy. After slavery was abolished, many ways were devised to guarantee that cheap black labor would still be available, whether it was organizing the Ku Klux Klan, passing Jim Crow laws in the South, or recruiting southern blacks to replace striking white workers in meatpacking in Kansas City and Omaha. In the novel the impact of greed on the morality of a society is acted out in the pursuit of oil. In the twentieth century, oil plays a significant role in the life of the Great Plains, from Texas to North Dakota. Tulsa once owned the title of Oil Capital of the World, and today the lust for oil still drives the state of Oklahoma to frack its way up to 3,300 earthquakes in 2015, 907 of which were 3 plus on the Richter scale.

The power structure that protects the oil industry and the machinations of oil-hungry men like Franklin Dedmeyer helps to create a community that spawns violence and twists law. Althea's socially polite and generous husband conducts his oil business with deceit and fraud. The land on which he finds oil belongs to an elderly black woman, Iola Bloodgood Tiger. Her

Creek husband had received an allotment of land in the Indian Territory as provided to Native Americans under the Dawes Act of 1887. When Iola does not want to sign the lease of her land to Dedmeyer and his associates, Althea's brother, Japheth, dynamites her house. When she disappears, Dedmeyer forges the lease to steal her land and plots ways to cheat his associates of their partnership in the deal. His associates, including the pathologically evil Japheth, also have their own plots to get more than their share.

Through Iola Tiger, Askew connects greed for material wealth, violence against African Americans, and the same drive for land that massacred Native Americans and herded them onto reservations. The oil-rich class is also deeply implicated in Klan activities and the control of government and policing necessary to run a corrupt white society at the expense of justice and respect for other races. At a masquerade party for Tulsa's oil-wealthy society, Japheth wears a noose around his neck and paints his face half-white and half-black, reminding all of the recent lynching of the white Roy Belton and the black Everett Candler. The black serving staff disappears when they see him, and the white crowd thinks it an unfit subject for a party but soon, like Althea, "seal[s] its mind over the vulgar invasion that had pierced the room."

The lynching of Roy Belton reminds an anxious black community of what whites will do to them if they cross the prescribed racial lines. Graceful's family fears for the safety of her brother, T.J., though it will be her twelve-year-old sister who later is killed in the riot. During the ride out on the prairie to hide T.J., Graceful is filled "with dread and loathing, with the cold beginnings of hatred" at every white face they pass. The journey is one in which "all that she'[s] held away from herself before [becomes] fully present." Instead of dismissing all uncomfortable recollections, as Althea does, Graceful's life depends on constantly remembering them.

The arrival of Japheth in Tulsa changes everything for Althea and Graceful. The first night he is in the Dedmeyer house, he goes to the maid's room and rapes Graceful. Soon afterward, he reveals his sister's past to her husband and his associates. Japheth's actions strip both women of the self-protections with which they had sought to insulate themselves from the exposure of their silenced lives. In a second graphic birth scene, Althea helps Graceful deliver the baby. The Whiteside families are now tied together, since Graceful's son is also Althea's nephew. There can be no joy or recognition in the connection, however, as it derives from the violence of a racist rape.

The gulf in understanding between blacks and whites is strikingly portrayed when Althea, in a panic to have Graceful with her, decides to go get her by walking to her home in Greenwood, or Little Africa, as the white people call it. In her good clothes and high heels, she soon is disoriented, surrounded by black people, hot and thirsty, and wincing in pain from shoes that have rubbed her heels raw. Looking for help, she goes into the office of the *Tulsa Star*, not knowing that it is a black newspaper or that its editor is an educated black man, Albert J. Smitherman, another historical figure who enters the novel as a character. Even worse, Althea has no perception of the danger she is creating for Mr. Smitherman and his pressman by her presence as a distraught white woman in his office, falsely claiming that she had been chased by black men.

The two men are afraid to throw this sobbing white woman out of the office and afraid to do as she asks, which is to drive her to Graceful's house. The only safe way for a black man and a white woman to be in a car together is for him to be chauffeuring on the front seat with the proverbial Miss Daisy in the back seat, a demeaning role that Mr. Smitherman has spent a lifetime trying to escape. As late as 1965, white civil rights worker Viola Liuzzo was driving her black companion from Selma to Montgomery when Alabama Klansmen opened fire on them and killed Liuzzo. A white woman who consorted with blacks was considered to have surrendered her claims to be protected by white men.

When armed bands of whites begin moving through Greenwood, shooting and burning homes and businesses, Graceful insists on taking her baby and going home to help her mother and siblings. Althea insists on accompanying her. Althea thinks that, as a white woman, she will be safe, and she dresses Graceful up as though she were a white lady, to protect her from the mob. The half-white, half-black baby is draped in blankets. The women's clothing offers no more real distinction between them as members of the human family than does the color of their skin, and the baby is literally kin to both. Althea suddenly realizes that her white skin will not save her if the crowd of angry men thinks the dark baby she holds is hers.

In both the literal and the symbolic sense, this journey across the color line of Tulsa will strip both women of all the trappings of their assumed racial and social identities. Both women become victims of the riot. White men assault Graceful when they discover she is a black woman in a white lady's clothing, stripping her breasts bare and threatening her life. Althea steps forward and demands that the mob stop, insisting that they leave her alone, crying: "She works for me!" When Japheth steps from the crowd, Graceful screams, but it is Althea he is after. He douses her in gasoline and lights a match. Both brother and sister are engulfed in flames. Only the quick action of the young black man who is in love with Graceful saves Althea's life. No one moves to help Japheth, however, and his body is soon as charred as that of the black man's he had earlier burned.

Althea's journey through Tulsa teaches her that both blacks and whites are "kin to me," literally as Whitesides and symbolically as human beings. Both races want to live in the promised land, and their essential kinship is a theme of the black minister, who reminds his congregation that the name "Beulah," the promised land of Israel in the Old Testament, meant "married." "We married to the Whiteman . . . the Whiteman is married to the Negro just as well," he preaches, and no matter how much they might want to divorce each other, it is not God's will: "We got to *deal* with the Whiteman here in Beulah." The "white side" of that truth is that whites must learn to deal with blacks as well. The races must enter the promised land together or not at all.

The novel notes that "regret is not repentance," as "repentance owns its part . . . [and] is at once sorrow and self-knowledge and a changing of the mind." Violence such as the 1921 race riot does not happen because good intentions run aground, and feeling sorry about it is just "sentiment" and "mean[s] nothing, stop[s] nothing." Althea has learned to see Graceful as a woman, but she tells her, "It's not me! . . . I didn't do any of this." Her painful experiences in the riot deepen her feelings for Graceful and her child, but her new awareness does not extend to altering any conventions of social practice. In a sad moment of goodbye to Graceful and her new husband, who saved Althea's life, Althea thinks momentarily about saying thank you to him, and concludes that "if they had not been colored she would have invited them into the parlor."

Oilmen stealing land once allotted to Native Americans, white employers exploiting black labor, one group of people demonizing another, one group building a culture by destroying that of another group, the double standards of the law, the double standards for women, the disdain for the poor—all the concerns of *Fire in Beulah* have their parallels and repetitions in the history of the Great Plains and its literary representations. From the massacre at Wounded Knee to the annihilation of Greenwood in Oklahoma, from Beret Holm's hostility toward the Irish or the town of Black Hawk's stigmatization of the hired girls, the literature of the Great Plains includes the dark side that connects plains history to the rest of America. Cities crystalize and concentrate the woe from "having wanted, wanted, wanted" more than was rightfully one's own. Mobs such as the four thousand that lynched Will Brown in Omaha in 1919 or the even-larger mob that burned and murdered in the Tulsa riot tended to occur in large population centers. These things happened in cities, where they make headlines and history books. Less well known and smaller in scope, discriminatory attitudes and actions have been part of the story of the Great Plains from the first settlers and in the smallest rural communities.

These novels give us a picture of city life that is mainly grim and dangerous. Today, almost all of the cities on the plains, or at least some sections of them, are considered especially attractive places to live and work. Omaha, Minneapolis, Tulsa, Kansas City and Overland Park, Denver, Fargo, and Sioux Falls regularly rank highly on various lists of most-livable cities, though most of them still contain large areas of intense poverty. Ironically, the racial and ethnic heterogeneity that stirred some of the strongest resistance and deadly violence is now often a cultural and economic asset. The split between urban and rural perspectives continues to widen as the population shifts to the cities. Politically, plains cities are the bluest spots in their red states, and new immigrants, who include such diverse groups as Sudanese and Latin and South Americans, contribute to over a hundred different languages spoken there. To realize their bright futures, the cities will need to remember that to enter Beulah, the promised land, the people must recognize that all are "married" to each other and must go together.

CHAPTER SEVEN

The Circle toward Home

You Can't Go Home Again, said Thomas Wolfe. Morag wonders
now if it may be the reverse which is true. You have to go home
again, in some way or other.
—Margaret Laurence, *The Diviners*

In our postmodern world, the question of "Where is home?"
challenges all the traditional answers. The definitions of "family"
and "place" are increasingly fluid as we seek to find home and
family in our disjointed, diverse, and highly mobile modern
life. The answers are not always in genealogy or geography,
religion or politics. The question of "home" is as thorny on the
Great Plains as it is anywhere. The region was heavily settled
by immigrants for whom home was another country and a
different language. The Native tribes who were at home on
the plains were driven into a form of exile within reservations
and schooled to annihilate their language and religious beliefs.
The rural life built around homesteads, family farms, and small
towns is dying in a major shift in population to urban settings.
Today only about 2 percent of the U.S. population actually
farms. Even Mom and Dad and grandparents have left the
farm. The Scandinavians, Germans, Irish, and Czechs who
once had distinct local cultures are largely assimilated into the
general population and mainly celebrate their heritage with
old-country holiday traditions. In the cities, we eat everyone's

ethnic foods, collapse religious distinctions into unity churches without doctrinal history, and give distinctly ethnic names like Sean and Megan to children with no Irish or Welsh ancestry. What binds and defines us is clearly more complex than a particular acreage, a hometown, or the family relations of the genealogical chart.

The question of home on the contemporary Great Plains lies at the heart of some of the best work of its most distinguished contemporary writers. Three novelists and one poet from the Great Plains have achieved national and international reputations for their writings about the region in the last thirty or so years. Ted Kooser of Nebraska was the first poet from the Great Plains to be named poet laureate of the United States. Novelists Margaret Laurence of Manitoba, Louise Erdrich of North Dakota, and Kent Haruf of Colorado have all won many prestigious national awards for their fiction. Place and the past are inescapable for them, but defining "home" and "family" is not simple or always comforting. Kooser, like the eminent modernist poet Wallace Stevens, juggled a corporate career as an insurance executive in Lincoln with a life of writing from the "Bohemian Alps" of rural Nebraska's barely rolling hills. Haruf's fictional town of Holt lies on the high plains in eastern Colorado. "Home" and "family" in Holt may be turned upside down, and Haruf finds their living essence in unexpected places and people. Erdrich explores the tragedies of the past that linger in the racially mixed lives of the whites and Native Americans of North Dakota. Laurence creates the town of Manawaka in her native province of Manitoba, but returning there requires multiple relocations of place and transformations of family.

Kooser was born in Ames, Iowa, in 1939 and studied at Iowa State and the University of Nebraska–Lincoln. He published his first book of poetry in 1969 but worked for many years in insurance, becoming a vice president at Lincoln Benefit Life

Fig. 17. Ted Kooser, poet laureate of the United States, at home with his dogs. Photograph by Jon Huminston. Courtesy of *Nebraska Magazine* 100, no. 4 (Winter 2004)

Company. He lives in the country near Garland, Nebraska, and is Presidential Professor at the University of Nebraska.

Some critics describe him as an elegist, a poet rooted in one place whose subject is a simple way of life that is vanishing. That oversimplifies his subjects and misinterprets what his poetry accomplishes. The joy and beauty in Kooser's poetry is the richness of life he finds in ordinary things and people and the absolute respect with which he approaches them. His subject is the familiar world, which offers us more human complexity and wonders of life than we normally take time to see. The artist Edgar Degas once said, "Art is not what you see, but what you make others see." Kooser's art makes us see, not just what he has seen, but what we can see for ourselves. The precision of detail and immediacy of experience give readers their own access to the scene, and the poet knows when to stop and let us do the rest of the work.

The poem "Pearl" from Kooser's Pulitzer Prize–winning collection, *Delights and Shadows* (2004), is a fine example of a poem about a sad but familiar moment of shared love and grief. It captures the power of attachment, death, and memory in our lives. Pearl is an elderly cousin, ninety years old, and the speaker has driven a hundred miles to tell Pearl of his mother's death. When he knocks on her door, he identifies himself:

> "Pearl,
> it's Ted. It's Vera's boy," and my voice broke,
> for it came to me, nearly sixty, I was still
> my mother's boy, that boy for the rest of my life.

Pearl, his mother's childhood playmate, is like his mother in age, kinship, and memory. As they talk, he sees in her both his mother who still lives inside him and the divide of death that has taken her and is approaching Pearl. Pearl tells him that she is not well herself, that she has "started seeing people who aren't here." He looks where she has pointed to one of these apparitions but sees nothing. She tells him these ghostly figures are making "lists of everything I own." The conversation turns to other things: "There were some stories / we laughed a little over, and I wept a little / and then it was time for me to go." As the door closes on him, he knows the unseen figures are resuming their inventory of all Pearl's earthly goods.

The surface details of this poem are wonderfully ordinary, from Pearl's "blue cardigan buttoned over a housedress" to the cup of instant coffee she fixes for him and the quiet conversation remembering a time these young girls played tricks on Aunt Mabel. In the face of Pearl's extraordinary revelation of her spectral visitors, "Ted" tries to keep the conversation in the mundane world by asking what the doctor says. When she dismissively says of her doctor, "He's not much good," Ted lamely suggests, "But surely there's medicine." With grace for his lack of understanding, Pearl says, "Maybe so." Then there is "a pause that fill[s] the room." This delicate poem reveals in its silences and subtleties that the poet sees more than he articulates to Pearl. In their last goodbye, Ted does not mention the visitors who are taking everything from her world. He sensibly tells her to take care of herself and see a real medical doctor, but their "warm bony hands" join with "the light hands / of the shadows that reached to touch [them] but / drew back." Kooser's genius is to give us enough details to bring us into the room and enough silence to grant us the moment of personal perception.

One of my favorite poems by Kooser is "Christmas Mail." Writing a fresh and original poem about Christmas—one that dares include such hackneyed seasonal iconography as angels, a star, a lamb, wise men, and shepherds—is a challenge few would try. Both T. S. Eliot and W. B. Yeats succeeded in doing so but with all the high seriousness and tradition of the journey of the magi who find in the stable "the uncontrollable mystery on the bestial floor." Kooser does it with a rural mail carrier delivering Christmas cards. I present the poem in full here with Kooser's generous permission:

CHRISTMAS MAIL

Cards in each mailbox,
angel, manger, star and lamb,
as the rural carrier,
driving the snowy roads,
hears from her bundles
the plaintive bleating of sheep,
the shuffle of sandal,
the clopping of camels.
At stop after stop,
she opens the little tin door
and places deep in the shadows
the shepherds and wise men,
the donkeys lank and weary,
the cow who chews and muses.
And from her Styrofoam cup,
white as a star and perched
on the dashboard, leading her
ever into the distance,
there is a hint of hazelnut,
and then a touch of myrrh.

For this mail carrier, making her rounds alone on the snowy road, the mystery of Christmas comes to life with every card she places in the tin mailboxes on her route. In her imagination each card brings the sights and sounds of the manger until even the scent of myrrh fills the air. The poem both evokes a magical moment and plays with the conventions that could, if the spirit were not real for her, make it satiric. "The cow who chews and muses" offers up a rhyme that is both apt and amusing. Cows are ruminants, and "to ruminate" is "to muse." "Angel, manger, star and lamb" may evoke the rhyme and rhythm of a child's verse. And that "Styrofoam cup, / white as a star," gives off "a hint of hazelnut," though probably not from *Star*buck's. But the spirit is alive in her, and her imagination of the mail has made incarnate the meaning of Christmas. Kooser's poem shows us that no setting is too lowly, no experience too mundane to be the place where meaning may be created through the power of imaginative insight.

In this time in which cancer touches almost everyone in some way, Kooser's "At the Cancer Clinic" may be the poem that has resonated with the most readers. The poem grew out of his own experience as a cancer patient and his observations of others in similar situations.

AT THE CANCER CLINIC

She is being helped toward the open door
that leads to the examining rooms
by two young women I take to be her sisters.
Each bends to the weight of an arm
and steps with the straight, tough bearing
of courage. At what must seem to be
a great distance, a nurse holds the door,
smiling and calling encouragement.
How patient she is in the crisp white sails
of her clothes. The sick woman
peers from under her funny knit cap
to watch each foot swing scuffling forward
and take its turn under her weight.
There is no restlessness or impatience
or anger anywhere in sight. Grace

fills the clean mold of this moment
and all the shuffling magazines grow still.

From *Delights and Shadows*

Readers who know prosody will admire the delicate but steady underlying rhythms of the iambs, trochees, and anapests that reflect the rhythm of the woman's measured walk across the room. Like many of Kooser's best poems, however, the meaning needs no explication. The details manifest the presence of love, courage, and suffering that envelop the woman in her sisters' arms and that everyone else in the room recognizes in her and in themselves.

In Kooser's poetry the people and places of the Great Plains are alive with the richness of their common humanity and the joys and sorrows that mark off the parts of our lives. Rather than writing an elegy for the plains, Kooser writes the poetry of attachment. His attachment is to the people in his family and the small towns near his home, the road by his house and the changing of the seasons, the snow in the fields and the spring rain. They are the source of constant "delights and shadows." In "On the Road," the poet spots a Frostian "pebble of quartz, / one drop of the earth's milk," which he "could almost see through ... / into the grand explanation." Unlike Robert Frost, who keeps trying to look into the well of mystery in search of "for once, then, something," Kooser keeps his eyes on the road, forward through the landscapes he embraces as home. Kooser's revelations are in local places and ordinary people. He does not need "the grand explanation" of cosmic mystery that Frost hopes to see in nature. Reflecting on the stone, Kooser writes, "something told me, / put it back and keep walking."

Kooser would no doubt recognize the people in the fictional world of Kent Haruf's Holt, Colorado. Haruf (1943–2014) was born in Pueblo, Colorado, and educated at Nebraska

Wesleyan University and the Iowa Writers' Workshop. All six of his novels are set in his fictional small town of Holt in the high plains of eastern Colorado. The titles of his novels often imply something traditionally religious, but the books find grace in secular settings and good-hearted people. *Plainsong* (1999) takes its title from both the geographic locale and the musical form of an unaccompanied liturgical chant. *Eventide* (2004) continues the stories of characters from *Plainsong*. His last novel, *Our Souls at Night*, appeared in 2015 after his death.

Plainsong tells several loosely entwined stories. Victoria Roubideaux is a teenager who has perhaps the cruelest mother on the plains. When her angry mother finds out that Victoria is pregnant, she locks her out of the house, permanently, with only the thin clothes on her back and the change in her purse. With this dramatic and unrelenting loss of home, the girl turns, in desperation, to one of her high school teachers, Maggie Jones, for shelter. Maggie helps place Victoria with two elderly bachelors, the McPheron brothers, who live alone on a farm seventeen miles from town. In a related story, Maggie's colleague and friend, Tom Guthrie, is dealing with a self-involved wife who has left him with their two boys, Ike and Bobby, who are hurt and puzzled by their mother's absence. These lives come together in comfort and love as they all try to get through the difficulties of life as decent people who can help each other.

The center of the novel is the story of Victoria and Raymond and Harold McPheron. These bachelor brothers tend their cattle and stay too much to themselves. Their household is perhaps the most unlikely home that one could imagine for this girl, but all three of them are transformed by the unexpected kindness and love that grow on all sides. Haruf's gift with humor shows as we watch the two old men try to figure out how to make this troubled young girl "feel a little at home." When they learn from Maggie that Victoria reports "they don't talk," they realize that they need to learn how to converse with the girl. On their first attempt, after listening to the farm report on the radio, they ask this seventeen-year-old what she thinks "of the market": "Buy or sell, would you say." She sees the kindness in their effort to talk and responds by asking them to "explain it to [her]." The long conversation that follows about soybeans and pork bellies is classic in its unconscious quirkiness and the touching interest of all parties to communicate on this topic.

The growing ties of affection between Victoria and the McPherons are fully affirmed when the brothers decide to try to lift her out of the Christmas doldrums by taking her shopping for a baby crib. Like the most indulgent of grandfathers, they buy the best crib in the furniture store, and she is overwhelmed with their generosity. That night, for the first time, she serves dinner in the kitchen instead of the formal dining room. "It seems homier," she says. Not all will go well for Victoria as the novel continues, but the sense of home she finds this night will stay with her and bring her back to the brothers.

The Guthrie boys, Ike and Bobby, who are ten and nine years old, also have troubles at home. They do not understand why their mother has left home and does not plan to come back. Their serious eyes study the adults around them, and their ability to see who is kind and will ease their hurting is acute. One such person is Mrs. Stern, a cigarette-smoking old woman who wears bright-red lipstick. She is on their newspaper route, and she lives alone in the world in rented rooms. When they go to collect every Saturday morning, she makes them sit down and talk to her for a while before she pays them. They tell her that their mother has left, and she tells them that she lost her son in the war. Soon they visit her when it is not collection day.

None of them has much of a home left, but they are among those who, for a short time, improvise on its comforts.

Haruf's style is high risk, because it would be so easy for the simplicity of it to seem simplistic and for the grace and decency of people like the McPherons, Victoria, Mrs. Stern, and Ike and Bobby to be sentimentalized or overburdened with "higher" meanings. In novel after novel, he succeeds in giving us people in need who find each other, maybe not for a lifetime, but for a while, making a reality of home where no one has a reason to expect it. Holt is not without its violence, dishonesty, and cowardice; but those things never outweigh the potential for goodness in humanity that comforts our suffering and overlooks our failures.

Louise Erdrich's fictional world, set in and around the Turtle Mountain Chippewa reservation in North Dakota, is burdened with a history that makes forgiveness difficult and forgetting impossible. With a dozen fine novels, Erdrich has won a place among the best American novelists of the contemporary period. In 1954 in Little Falls, Minnesota, Erdrich was born to a white father and an Ojibwe (Chippewa) mother descended from Patrick Gourneau, a noted tribal chairman. Erdrich's parents were both teachers at an Indian boarding school in Wahpeton, North Dakota. *The Plague of Doves* (2008) weaves a complicated story over time, told through multiple narratives and generations, that we slowly fit together. The complications make definitions of victims and villains, Indian and white, increasingly difficult to categorize. Without clear lines of responsibility and grievance, vengeance and justice are impossible to mete out.

The Plague of Doves is based on a true incident in North Dakota history of an 1897 lynching that followed the murder of an entire family. In revenge, a group of white men hanged three innocent Native Americans, including a thirteen-year-old boy. In the novel the lynching is in 1911, and in the 1970s both

Native Americans and whites are still alive who know truths still hidden about the incident. Their children and grandchildren are connected in the many ways a small community can become over three generations. Mainly white and just within the reservation, the town of Pluto is itself the constant reminder of past injustices that still determine the parameters of the present. Evelina Harp, the granddaughter of Mooshum Milk, the one Native American hanged who was cut down before he died, must come to terms with the lynching and the secrets that remain hidden about that fateful incident. As the novel unfolds, we hear the stories of Evelina, her friend Corwin Peace, Billy Peace, and several others related to the victims or the perpetrators.

One thing the Native people cover up is the depth of their sorrow about the loss of their land. When asked for a town history about how Pluto came to be within the reservation, Mooshum rephrases the question: "What you are asking . . . is how was it stolen? How has this great thievery become acceptable? How do we live right here beside you, knowing what we lost and how you took it?" The question, "How do we live right here beside you [with such tragic knowledge]?" is central to the many narratives in the book. The loss of the land haunts the Native people, and both races are haunted by the lynching of the three innocent Indians. No one was ever arrested for participating in the lynching, though their identities were known to many, including the sheriff.

Many people know or tell part of the story, and it reverberates differently with various narrators. In order to unfold the details of the story, Erdrich assigns the narrative to different people. The narrative structure reminds one of Faulkner's *Absalom, Absalom!*, another tragic story of cruel oppression (slavery) and the generational consequences of race hatred and miscegenation. It is a complicated structure, but the complexities themselves illustrate the many repercussions of the lynching in Pluto's history. The narrative structure also allows Erdrich to portray in detail a cast of exceptional characters whose own stories give this novel the depth of interest that makes the murders at its center personal in the lives of those who are touched by them.

Mooshum, Evelina's grandfather, tells her the first story that reveals the complicated genealogy of the participants and their descendants. Her perception of everyone around her is changed as she realizes that her most beloved teacher, Sister Mary Anita, is a Buckendorf and that Emil Buckendorf participated in the lynching. Even Evelina's Chippewa grandmother, Junesse, was fathered by Eugene Wildstrand, another of the four white men who did the actual lynching. Evelina's boyfriend, Corwin Peace, is descended from both the lynched Cuthbert Peace and the lyncher Wildstrand. What Mooshum does not tell Evelina is his own guilty part in the story. The further we get into the novel, the more connections emerge between Indian and white, the victims and those who lynched them.

The connections are so extensive that readers may feel they need a genealogical map to keep the characters straight. Evelina is driven to create one: "I traced the blood history of the murders through my classmates and friends until I could draw out elaborate spider webs of lines and intersecting circles." Even Erdrich finally created family trees after her readers kept showing her the ones they had drawn! The complex narrative maintains the suspense of the novel as we join the characters in trying to piece together what happened and how this tragedy is still working out. As one character says, "Nothing that happens, *nothing*, is not connected here by blood." More importantly, the interlacing bloodlines and conflicting views of guilt and innocence speak to the tension between a troubled national history of racism and prejudice and the idealistic principles in our founding documents of democracy and equality.

E pluribus unum ("out of many, one") is the American national motto, which is inscribed on every U.S. coin, but "the blood history" that runs through the town of Pluto is a microcosm of our nation's tragic quest for unity in diversity. By the novel's end, much of the story has been illuminated, but resolution is elusive. Even the story is subject to the slow erasure of memory that accompanies the town's gradual demise. For those descended from both the victims and the perpetrators, learning to embrace the family bonds in forgiveness is essential to finding a way to "live right here . . . , knowing." In *The Round House* (2012) Erdrich moves the story forward about fifteen years to 1988 when yet another generation of young people struggle to find justice on the reservation.

The Round House builds on the legal complexities of tribal jurisdiction and state and federal jurisdiction that can keep even those guilty of horrendous crimes from being prosecuted. Judge Coutts and his thirteen-year-old son, Joe, descendants of the Joseph Coutts who was hanged, must find a way to achieve justice for the brutal rape of their wife and mother, who is a descendant of Mooshum Milk, the one who survived the hanging. The perpetrator of the rape is a descendent of the lynching party. That quest for justice is still haunted by the 1911 murders of whites and Indians. As Joe says, "We know the families of the men who were hanged. We know the families of the men who hanged them. We even know our people were innocent of the crime they were hung for." The suspense and terror at the heart of this novel make it hard to put down, and the reader's ideas of justice and law are challenged by the strong emotions this story evokes.

Many of the racial themes in Erdrich's novels also play a role in Margaret Laurence's *The Diviners* (1974), but this time they appear in the context of the Canadian Prairies. Born in Neepawa, Manitoba, Laurence (1926–87) creates the fictional town of Manawaka, which is drawn from her life in Neepawa. *The Diviners* is the fifth and last novel in a series set in Manawaka. The novel also reflects much of Laurence's own life in the story of Morag Gunn, a novelist reared by guardians of Scot descent. Morag leaves home and marries her professor from England but leaves him and has a child with a Métis man from Manawaka. Morag's development takes us through the conflicts of class and race in modern Canada, the quest for a feminist identity, love of the harsh but beautiful land, and the need to escape all that Manawaka represents in order to find what should be cherished. The novel takes Morag from age five to forty-seven in a narrative that moves back and forth in time through photographs, imagined "Memorybank movies," and mythic stories from both the Indian and Scot heritages of the area. *The Diviners* is both Laurence's best work and, in many people's opinion, the finest Canadian novel yet written.

Morag Gunn tries to erase her past in Manawaka when she goes to the university in Winnipeg and marries her professor. She winds up hating this new life and finally has to admit that her efforts to escape the past have failed: "I never forgot any of it. It was always there." Her past is rich with meaning; but as a young woman, she remembers mainly the pain and embarrassment. When her parents both died of polio, her father gave her into the guardianship of an army buddy, Christie Logan. Christie and his wife, Prin, live in quite humble circumstances, as he is the garbage collector for Manawaka. The dump, called the "Nuisance Grounds," is the source of most of the clothing and furniture in their messy and odoriferous home. Morag's guardians love her, but Christie usually smells like the dump, and Prin is obese and seems slow-witted. At school Morag wears long, baggy dresses and is teased about her family. In high school she gets a job and buys some stylish clothes. Still, at church with Prin, the "best people" will not say "Good morning" to them. As a teenager, she sometimes feels she "hates" Christie, and "she loves Prin, but can no longer bear to be seen with her in public."

Christie is nobody's fool, or rather, he is a Shakespearean wise fool. His colorful tales of the adventures of Piper Gunn, his legendary hero who led the Gunn clan from Scotland to Manitoba, spark Morag's interest in stories and the nature of history. Many Scots emigrated to Canada in the nineteenth century when Highland farmers were evicted in a plan to change the agriculture into a sheep economy. These Highland Clearances dispersed the clans and destroyed much of Scottish-Gaelic culture. Christie's tales of Piper Gunn assert that his "kin and clan are as good as theirs any day of the week," and they are vital to his identity, as they become, too, for Morag. Morag begins to write her feminist alternative versions of Christie's stories. In school she learns yet another, official version, which is less heroic than Christie's mythic saga. Later in life, as she reclaims her past, Morag will think, "A popular misconception is that we can't change the past—everyone is constantly changing their own past, recalling it, revising it. What really happened? A meaningless question. But one I keep trying to answer, knowing there is no answer."

Though Christie is the teller of tales par excellence (he can even "read" stories in the garbage he collects), the local Métis people have their own mythic stories of the past. Morag's first lover and father of her daughter, Pique, is Jules Tonnerre, part French, part Indian (originally Bois Brules). His family's stories of Rider Tonnerre cast him as a great horseman whose white stallion emerged from a haunted lake. Rider successfully fought the *Anglais* and *Arkanys* (the English and the Scots—men from Orkney). This legend has it that as an old man, Rider joins a mythically powerful Louis Riel to stop the *Anglais* from taking the land away from the Métis.

Louis Riel (1844–85) was a Métis leader and central figure in the history of Manitoba. He also appears in Erdrich's fiction. Riel led a rebellion against British rule and then fled to Montana, where he actually became an American citizen. He returned to Canada to lead another effort to end British rule and was eventually hanged for treason. Christie has his own version of how Louis Riel and his "halfbreeds" took Fort Garry. In Christie's account Piper Gunn and his sons took back Fort Garry before "them bloody Sassenachs" (the English) even arrived! When he tells his version to Morag, who learned about Riel and the uprising in school, she says, "Oh Christie! They didn't. We took it in History."

Christie's stories and the fluency of his distinct verbal style create a culture that fosters Morag's desire to write stories. She knows early that she wants to write, but it is only in college that she begins to believe that she might be a good writer. Unfortunately, Brooke Skelton, her university professor and husband, wants her to be a decorative companion, not a serious writer. Skelton liked that Morag never brought up her past and that, initially, she seemed malleable. Morag learns the ways of an educated, fashionable faculty wife, and he treats her like a pet, calling her "little one" and "child." Her intense anger at not being taken seriously as an adult and a writer eventually explodes the relationship. The wife he wants her to be is an "external self" she comes to hate. She stops going to the hairdresser—"I don't want to look like that"—and when Morag leaves Skelton, she rents a "room of her own" in conscious affinity with Virginia Woolf.

Questions of home and identity become more pressing after Morag ends her marriage and is pregnant with Pique, fathered by Jules Tonnerre. Pique will experience the same kind of racial prejudice in school as her Métis father had, and she will learn the many stories of Piper Gunn her mother knows. Morag settles in Vancouver to have her child; but even as she rides the train out of the prairie, she thinks, "People who'd never lived hereabouts always imagined it was dull, bleak, hundreds of miles of nothing. They didn't know. They didn't know the renewal that came out of the dead cold."

Slowly Morag discovers who her true family is and what she needs to create a home for herself and Pique. While living several years in England, she plans a trip to Scotland to see Sutherland, where Piper Gunn had lived. At the last minute, she realizes that she does not need to go to the real Sutherland, that Christie's myths "are [her] reality": "I always thought it was the land of my ancestor, but it is not." Her land is "Christie's real country," where she was born. When she gets a telegram that Christie is dying, she tells her daughter that they are "going back home." Morag arrives in time to tell Christie, "You've been my father to me." After years of trying to escape her past, in her writing, in her marriage, in Vancouver, in London, Morag circles back home. Morag thought that she could leave home, but then "found the whole town was inside [her] head, for as long as [she would] live."

Writing was Morag's divining tool, which she used to find the sources that have given meaning to being. Her daughter, Pique, like her father, has her divining tool in music. To find family and home, each must create it. Pique must also return to Manawaka and then to Galloping Mountain, the mythic home of the Tonnerres. Pique's family is as unconventional as Morag's was, her Métis father a symbol of both the mixed blood and mixed cultures that are the ink in which Manawaka's, and Canada's, history is written. Just as the hunting knife that once belonged to Jules's father wound up with Christie, who gave it to Morag, who gave it to Jules, who gives it at last to Pique, the Scottish plaid pin made its way to Jules's hands and then to Morag's, who will leave it to Pique. At the end, both the Scot's pin and the Métis's knife may be said rightly to belong within the family.

One constant throughout the novel is the river that runs both ways. It flows north to south, but winds from the south push the waves against the current. Morag finally buys a log house on the river at McConnell's Landing. The house is an original homestead nearly one hundred years old. Past and future are in this place, but they are like the river, running both ways, taking Morag away and bringing her back. "History" is many stories, and past and future are not neatly divided. "Look ahead into the past, and back into the future, until the silence," is Morag's meditative thought about the nature of history and identity, about creating "home." Like the river, one's identity may be clear in the shallows, but further out, the deep water keeps "its life from sight." The writer's "gift, or portion of grace, or whatever it [is]," is a kind of divining magic that can help us to see the life that lives in the depths. Margaret Laurence's novel is abundant in its gift and its portion of grace.

Kooser, Haruf, Erdrich, and Laurence connect contemporary readers back to the land, to history, to family, and to home, but not in the old ways of pioneer days. The land is the expression of the beauty of earth, more under threat now than threatening. Today's task is to preserve the plains environment, not to exploit it. Its open spaces are a refuge from the city, not the terrifying emptiness that could drive one mad. The pioneers faced the challenge of surviving in a new land, but they did not feel the weight of history in the new place. That bloody history of conquest and death is alive today in places like Wounded Knee, Pine Ridge, Rosebud, and White Clay. The farmsteads and small towns are increasingly dysfunctional, but the cities on the Great Plains are rated among the best places to live or to raise a family. The idea of family is perhaps the most changed of all. The novels of Haruf, Erdrich, and Laurence illustrate that family is what one creates. The McPheron brothers, Victoria Roubideaux, and Katie are as real a family as anything in the Ingalls' little house on the prairie. Morag Gunn, foster daughter of Christie and Prin Logan; Pique, daughter of Morag and Jules, part Scot, part Indian, part French; and Royland, their good neighbor who grandfathers Pique, know that they are each other's family. Robert Frost once wrote, "Home is the place where, when you have to go there, / They have to take you in." But this is an ungenerous definition. These authors have implicitly revised it to say, "Home is the place where, when you have to go there, they *want* to take you in."

These Great Plains artists, from Black Elk and Rölvaag to Erdrich, have written the stories that help to define the place and what it means to live there. Holt, Colorado; Tulsa, Oklahoma; Pluto, North Dakota; Manawaka, Manitoba; Red Cloud, Nebraska—whether literal or fictional, all are places so real that we can point a finger to the exact spot on a map. These places are not alike, and yet we recognize them all as the plains. Just living on the plains is a climate adventure that unites all its residents. In Vancouver, Morag Gunn runs into an old friend from home who says, "We all head west, kiddo. We think it'll be heaven on earth—no forty below in winter, no blast furnace in summer, and mountains to look at, not just grain elevators . . . and every time we meet someone from back home we fall on their necks and weep."

The continuities in subject and setting between the writers of the early period, 1890–1940, and those from 1970–2014 are striking. Haruf's town of Holt recalls the quiet lives of Cather's many variations on Red Cloud, without her desire to escape it. Black Elk's account of the passing of the days of freedom on the plains to the confines of reservations is background for Erdrich's portrait of troubled life on the contemporary reservations. The abiding question of how to live together, knowing the tragedy of the past, illustrates how wrong the "solutions" of the victors have often been. Rölvaag's epic of the pioneer settlement of the Dakota Territory is background to Laurence's Manawaka, where Christie Logan rewrites history to make his Scottish ancestors the heroes who tamed the Canadian Prairies. Accompanying the success stories of building communities and finding wealth and power are the stories of injustices, racial discrimination, and exploitation. Lynching is also part of the Great Plains' history, though much effort has been expended to paper it over.

This book can offer only an introduction to the richness of literature on the Great Plains, with the hope that it may be the beginning of a long and fascinating companionship between the reader and the artists. It hardly allows us occasion to point toward today's writers who are continuing the traditions of their literary heritage. There is no shortage of fine work that can make a claim on our attention. Rudy Wiebe's *The Scorched-Wood People* and *The Temptations of Big Bear* have been among the most praised recent Canadian fiction. Jonis Agee's *The Weight of Dreams* is set in western Nebraska and explores the still-volatile relationships between whites and Native Americans. The late Jim Harrison's *Dalva*, one of his finest novels, is about a woman from the Great Plains who traces the history of the region. Ted Kooser believes that this book should be on the bookshelf beside *My Ántonia* and *Black Elk Speaks*. Karen Shoemaker's new novel, *The Meaning of Names*, has also won praise for her story about the prejudice against German Americans on the plains during World War I. These are only a few of the contemporary artists whose work addresses the region today. Every state and province in the plains has successful writers who are drawing on the legacy of plains literature. As Booker T. Washington once advised, "Cast down your bucket where you are."

The Great Plains may be facing its greatest challenge yet, with climate change and the growing scarcity of water. Ever since those hopeful homesteaders journeyed into the plains, perhaps believing that rain followed the plow or just that such hard work would not go unrewarded, the geography and climate of the region have posed its biggest threats. The white people shot the buffalo out from under the culture of the Native people, but now the descendants of those white settlers may be facing their own attacks on the viability of the culture they built in its place. Little towns dwindle, and corporate farming consumes the family farm. The descendants of farm families move to the cities for high-tech jobs and new lifestyles. The familiar conflicts go on between those seeking to protect the land and those who would extract its riches at any cost. Again we see images of Native Americans massed in North Dakota, their tents and tepees frozen in the snow, in scenes poignantly evocative of Wounded Knee. Government forces protect the oil pipeline, while Indians try to preserve the water and sacred land from pollution. The history of the Great Plains clearly has critical chapters in its story yet to unfold. As Margaret Laurence writes at the end of *The Diviners*, "Look ahead into the past, and back into the future, until the silence." The past and the future are the river that flows both ways, and it is the transport on which the literature of the Great Plains travels.

APPENDIX

Great Plains Literary Sites to Visit

Akta Lakota Museum and Cultural Center, Chamberlain, South Dakota

Bess Streeter Aldrich Home, Elmwood, Nebraska

John G. Neihardt Historic Site, Bancroft, Nebraska

John Hope Franklin Reconciliation Park and Museum, Tulsa, Oklahoma

Laura Ingalls Wilder Museum and Dugout Home, near Walnut Grove, Minnesota

Little House on the Prairie Museum, near Independence, Kansas

Margaret Laurence Home, Neepawa, Manitoba, Canada

Mari Sandoz High Plains Heritage Center, Chadron State College campus, Chadron, Nebraska

Ole Edvart Rölvaag Home, Northfield, Minnesota

Ole Edvart Rölvaag Writing Cabin, campus of Augustana College, Sioux Falls, South Dakota

Willa Cather Home and related sites, Red Cloud, Nebraska

Wounded Knee Museum, Wall, South Dakota

FURTHER READING

Anderson, Kathie Ryckman. *Dakota: The Literary Heritage of the Northern Prairie State*. Grand Forks: University of North Dakota Press, 1990.

Cather, Willa. *One of Ours*. New York: Vintage Classics, 1991.

——. *The Song of the Lark*. New York: Signet Classics, 2007.

Dick, Everett. *The Sod-House Frontier, 1854–1890: A Social History of the Northern Plains from the Creation of Kansas and Nebraska to the Admission of the Dakotas*. Lincoln NE: Johnsen, 1954.

Ellsworth, Scott. *Death in a Promised Land*. Baton Rouge: Louisiana State University Press, 1982.

Erdrich, Louise. *The Beet Queen*. New York: Bantam, 1987.

——. *Love Medicine*. New York: HarperCollins, 1993.

Friesen, Gerald. *The Canadian Prairies: A History*. Toronto: University of Toronto Press, 1987.

Garland, Hamlin. *Main-Travelled Roads*. New York: Signet Classics, 1962.

Greene, Jerome. *American Carnage: Wounded Knee, 1890*. Norman: University of Oklahoma Press, 2014.

Hada, Kenneth. "The Power to Undo Sin: Race, History and Literary Blackness in Rilla Askew's *Fire in Beulah*." *College Literature* 34, no. 4 (Fall 2007): 166–87.

Harrison, Jim. *Dalva*. New York: Washington Square Press, 1988.

Holler, Clyde, ed. *The Black Elk Reader*. Syracuse: Syracuse University Press, 2000.

Laurence, Margaret. *The Stone Angel*. London: Macmillan, 1964.

Limerick, Patricia Nelson. *The Legacy of Conquest: The Unbroken Past of the American West*. New York: Norton, 1987.

Luebke, Frederick C. "Ethnic Group Settlement on the Great Plains." *Western Historical Quarterly* 8 (1977): 405–30.

Maher, Susan Naramore. *Deep Map Country: Literary Cartography of the Great Plains*. Lincoln: University of Nebraska Press, 2014.

Micheaux, Oscar. *The Homesteader*. With an introduction by Learthen Dorsey. Lincoln: University of Nebraska Press, 1994.

Momaday, N. Scott. *House Made of Dawn*. New York: Harper and Row, 1968.

Moulton, Gary E., ed. *The Lewis and Clark Journals*. Abridged edition. Lincoln: University of Nebraska Press, 2003.

Murphy, John J. *Critical Essays on Willa Cather*. Boston: G. K. Hall, 1984.

Neihardt, John G. *The Twilight of the Sioux*. Vol. 2 of *A Cycle of the West*. Lincoln: University of Nebraska Press, 1971.

Nicholson, Colin, ed. *Critical Approaches to the Fiction of Margaret Laurence*. London: Macmillan Press, 1990.

O'Brien, Sharon. *The Emerging Voice*. New York: Oxford University Press, 1987.

——— , ed. *New Essays on* My Antonia. Cambridge: Cambridge University Press, 1999.

Olson, James C., and Ronald C. Naugle. *History of Nebraska*. 3rd ed. Lincoln: University of Nebraska Press, 1997.

Quantic, Diane D. *The Nature of the Place: A Study of Great Plains Fiction*. Lincoln: University of Nebraska Press, 1995.

Reigstad, Paul. *Rölvaag: His Life and Art*. Lincoln: University of Nebraska Press, 1972.

Reynolds, Guy. *Willa Cather in Context*. New York: St. Martin's Press, 1996.

Rosowski, Susan J., ed. *Approaches to Teaching* My Antonia. New York: Modern Language Association, 1989.

Sandoz, Mari. *Crazy Horse*. With an introduction by Vine Deloria Jr. Lincoln: University of Nebraska Press, 2008.

——— . *Old Jules*. Lincoln: University of Nebraska Press, 2005.

Simonson, Harold P. *Prairies Within: The Tragic Trilogy of Ole Rölvaag*. Seattle: University of Washington Press, 1987.

Skaggs, Merrill Maguire. *After the World Broke in Two: The Later Novels of Willa Cather*. Charlottesville: University Press of Virginia, 1990.

Stauffer, Helen Winter. *Mari Sandoz, Story Catcher of the Plains*. Lincoln: University of Nebraska Press, 1982.

Stegner, Wallace. *Where the Bluebird Sings to the Lemonade Springs: Living and Writing in the West*. New York: Modern Library Classics, 2002.

———. *Wolf Willow*. New York: Viking Press, 1962.

Stillwell, Mary K. *The Life and Poetry of Ted Kooser*. Lincoln: University of Nebraska Press, 2013.

Terkel, Studs. *Hard Times: An Oral History of the Great Depression*. New York: Pantheon, 1970.

Webb, Walter Prescott. *The Great Plains*. New York: Grosset and Dunlap, 1931.

Wishart, David J., ed. *Encyclopedia of the Great Plains*. Lincoln: University of Nebraska Press, 2007.

Zitkala-Ša. *American Indian Stories, Legends, and Other Writings*. Edited by Cathy N. Davidson and Ada Norris. New York: Penguin, 2003.

INDEX

employment *(continued)*
113–15, 124. *See also* economy;
meatpacking; migrant workers; prostitutes; unions
Encyclopedia of the Great Plains,
3–5, *4*
"The End of the First Cycle"
(Cather), 58–59
England, 142–44
Erdrich, Louise: background of,
137; literature of, 14, 17, 137–
40; on past and place, 128,
145, 146, 147; writing style of,
138–39
ethnicity: in *Capital City*, 97–
98; on Great Plains, 14–17,
42–43, 55, 58–59, 104, 106–7,
126–28; of migrant workers,
82–83; in *My Ántonia*, 67,
70–73; in Omaha, 109. *See
also* Bohemians; Czechs;
Norwegians; *specific countries*
Eureka. *See* Cleveland N D
Europe: Black Elk in, 32; immigrants from, 16, 19, 42, 58,
61–63, 80, 104, 109. *See also
specific countries*
Eventide (Haruf), 135

family life: in *Capital City*, 98–
99; Depression-era stresses
on, 90–92; in *Fire in Beulah*,
121–25; in *The Girl*, 115; of
humanity, 123–26, 134; in
metropolitan areas, 107–11; in
My Ántonia, 73–74; and social
class, 96; unconventional

representations of, 135–46. *See
also* home
Fargo N D, 103–4, 126
Farmers' Holiday Association, 81
Farmers' Union, 81
farming: in *Capital City*, 95–97;
decline of, 104, 106–10,
127, 145; discrimination in
communities of, 126; during
Great Depression, 80–93,
101–2; on Great Plains, 16,
46, 58–59, 62–63, 103–4, 142;
in *My Ántonia*, 69, 72; of
wheat, 86
Fascism, 94–98. *See also* politics
Faulkner, William, 55, 138
feminism, 113–14, 141, 142. *See
also* women
Fire in Beulah (Askew), 16, 104,
117–25
Five Civilized Tribes, 118
Fort Garry, 143
Fort Robinson, 31
Fort Scott K S, 113
Franklin, Kanewa, 16, 95–99
Frazer, Sir James G., 27
French and Indian War, 2–3. *See
also* violence
French Indians, 142
From Ritual to Romance
(Weston), 27
frontier, settling of: cultural
influence of, 2–3; and effect
on Indians, 19, 34, 41;
encouragement of, 9–10; by
ethnic groups, 42–45, 127;
experience of, 13–16, 48–49,

55; during Great Depression, 80–83; Indians' fear of, 7; literature about, 10–11, 14–17, 147; in Nebraska, 58–61; and social classes, 75–79. *See also* Great Plains; whites

Frost, Robert, 67, 134, 146

Fuller, Margaret, 8

Garretson SD, 44

Gelfant, Blanche, 63

gender: in *Bones of Plenty*, 92; on Great Plains, 15–16, 61; in *Lost Lady*, 75–78; in *My Ántonia*, 67, 68–73, 78; in *O Pioneers!*, 61–67, 78, 91. *See also* sexuality; women

Georgia, Worcester v., 18–19

Germany, 43, 67, 94–97, 101, 109, 127, 147

Ghost Dance, 33

Giants in the Earth (Rölvaag), 43, 45–51, 56

The Girl (Le Sueur), 16, 104, 111–17

Glacier National Park, 5

Going-to-the-Sun Road, 5

The Golden Bough (Frazer), 27

Gold Shirts, 95–99

Gourneau, Patrick, 137

The Grapes of Wrath (Steinbeck), 15–16, 81, 82, 85–86, 94

Great Depression: city life during, 107–8; effect of, on farmers, 80–86, 93; fear and anger during, 95, 100, 101; on Great Plains, 15–16, 100, 101;

literature about, 85–86, 90, 101. *See also* economy

Great Plains: boundaries of, 3–4; climate of, 5–6, 13, 15–16, 80–81, 107, 146, 148; as "home," 127, 134, 146; landscape of, 1–9, *2*, *4*, 12–15, 17, 46–49, 68–70, 141, 144, 145, 148; literature of, 8–17, 85–86, 101, 126, 146–48; metropolitan areas on, 103–6, 145–46; oil on, 121; population of, 7, 9–10, 14–19, 42–43, 48–49, 56–60; prejudice on, 97, 100, 117–26, 147; romanticization of, 73–74. *See also* frontier, settling of

Great Sioux Reservation, 30

Greene, Jerome, 19

Greenwood District, Tulsa, 117–20

Guthrie, Woody, 81

Hanson, William F., 36

Hard Times (Terkel), 95

Harper's, 36

Harrison, Jim, 147

Haruf, Kent: background of, 134–35; on past and place, 128, 145, 146; portrayal of small-town life by, 17, 104; writing style of, 135, 137

Hawthorne, Nathaniel, 8

The History of the Dividing Line betwixt Virginia and North Carolina (Byrd), 11

Hitler, Adolf, 97

Holbrook family, 16, 107–11

Discover the Great Plains, a series from the Center for Great Plains Studies and the University of Nebraska Press, offers concise introductions to the natural wonders, diverse cultures, history, and contemporary life of the Great Plains. To order or obtain more information on these or other University of Nebraska Press titles, visit nebraskapress.unl.edu.

CPSIA information can be obtained
at www.ICGtesting.com
Printed in the USA
LVOW03s1348230118
563634LV00004B/8/P